HOW

DEFEND THE

CATHOLIC

FAITH

THE CHIEF POINTS OF DIFFERENCE BETWEEN THE PROTESTANT AND CATHOLIC CREEDS

BY THE
REV. F. LAUN

AQUINAS
School of Theology and Philosophy

REMIGIUS LAFORT, S.T.D.
Censor

𝕴mprimatur

JOHN CARDINAL FARLEY
Archbishop of New York

NEW YORK, October 18, 1915

THE UNIVERSITY PRESS, CAMBRIDGE, U.S.A.

NEW YORK
JOSEPH F. WAGNER

EDITOR'S PREFACE

A THOROUGH discussion of the points of difference is what is chiefly required by *bona fide* inquirers from without the fold, and to such inquirers this book is dedicated. It is hoped that to such inquirers no expression in this book will appear aggressive. In the impersonal atmosphere of a book of this kind, plain speaking is required and permissible, but there was far from the mind of the author any intention to be unkind or uncharitable. The attacks upon erroneous belief should not be misunderstood to be attacks on erroneous believers.

Also to inquirers from within the fold this book will be helpful, in enlightening them upon important matters of faith, and in enabling them to enlighten others who, with a good will, ask them for information.

CONTENTS

CONTENTS

The Chief Points of Difference

BETWEEN THE CATHOLIC AND PROTESTANT CREEDS

I. WHERE IS THE TRUE DOCTRINE?

The Protestant Assertion. We call ourselves evangelical Christians, because we adhere to the teaching of the Gospel contained in Holy Scripture. After being long in obscurity, these saving truths were brought into prominence again by the Reformation.

The Catholic Reply. We Catholics believe and confess that Jesus Christ, the Son of God and our only Redeemer and Mediator, founded one holy Church which, being Christ's own institution, has in every age preserved the truths that He revealed, pure and inviolate.

We believe and confess that this Church neither is nor can be any other than the Catholic Church, which can prove itself to have been always the One, Holy, Catholic or universal, and Apostolic communion of those who hold the true faith in Christ.

The Catholic Church has ever adhered to the Gospel, which would have perished long ago but for the Church, whereas Protestantism dates only from the sixteenth century.

Dr. Martin Luther, the leader in the Reformation, did not bring to light truths that had been forgotten; what he did was to substitute his own opinions for ancient truths. He did not rediscover the Bible, but altered and expounded it to suit his own views, thus giving rise to many errors. He was not divinely commissioned, but assumed the right to judge and reform God's Church.

6

The Protestant Assertion. The Bible had long been almost forgotten, and in its place all kinds of innovations and all manner of false doctrine regarding the most important articles of faith had been accepted by the Church. These innovations and erroneous doctrines are still upheld by the Roman Catholic Church.

The Catholic Reply. Christ uttered the promises: "I am with you all days, even to the consummation of the world" (Matth. xxviii, 20), and: "The Spirit of truth . . . shall abide with you" (John xiv, 17, cf. xvi, 13). Hence the Gospel could never be lost, and the Catholic Church has preserved Christ's doctrine as the truth necessary to salvation not only in the letter, but in the spirit (2 Cor. iii, 6). With unerring decision she has detected and exposed all false teachers who adhered to the letter rather than to the spirit of Christ. She has never accepted any erroneous doctrine and, therefore, whoever asserts that she still upholds such doctrines, calumniates her.

The Protestant Assertion. The most important points upon which the Roman Catholic Church teaches false doctrines are the following: I. Holy Scripture; II. The Church and her authority; III. The forgiveness of sins; IV. Faith and good works; V. The worship of saints; VI. The Holy Eucharist.

These points will be dealt with individually in the following chapters.

COMMENTARY

If we as Catholics were to admit that the Holy Church, founded on earth by Christ, could ever have forgotten or lost His Gospel, we should be denying the truth of our Lord's own words. Far from forgetting the Gospel, the Church has made countless sacrifices in order to preserve the truths entrusted to her, and she has kept them intact down to the present day. It was she that gave the Holy Bible to Christians, and she has ever been its faithful guardian. She alone can know and testify to the character of the Bible, for she existed before it did and she alone was appointed by God to protect and interpret it. She knew the story of our Lord's life and knew all His doctrines before a word of them had been committed to writing; she used the *Our Father* before it could be read in St. Matthew's Gospel; she administered baptism and the other sacraments in conformity with Christ's instructions before any of the Apostles had compiled a record of them. Guided by the Holy Spirit she has ever been most vigilant to prevent any tampering with the word of God. She has preferred to undergo grievous persecution rather than tolerate any error in faith. Never have *any kinds of innovations devised by men*, and *false doctrines regarding the most important articles of faith* been accepted by the Catholic Church in place of God's holy word.

Thus it is a complete distortion of the truth for Protestants to declare that they are evangelical Christians because they adhere to the teaching of the Gospel, which, they assert, was and is ignored by the Catholic Church. The truth is rather that now for nearly two thousand years Catholics have loyally adhered to the Gospel teaching given by Christ to His Church and preserved in her by the Apostles and their successors. The Protestant Church came into existence only in the sixteenth century, and none of the tenets in which Protestantism differs from Catholicism can be shown to be based upon the Gospel of Christ.

Catholic Teaching Uniform

Protestants say that it is necessary to distinguish carefully between the genuinely Christian element in Catholicism, as it appears in the writings of many Catholic theologians, in some popular devotional works, and in the lives of some Catholics, and, on the other hand, the "Roman errors" which in the course of time have found their way into the Church, chiefly through the fault of the Popes, and which have recently gained the ascendency.

In answer to this statement we maintain that there is no difference at all between "genuinely Christian" and "Roman" Catholicism. Neither the Popes nor the much slandered Jesuits have another catechism than that in general use, nor do they teach other articles of faith, other morality, or another way to heaven than those inculcated

8

by the learned and edifying Catholic works extolled by Protestants. In every age there have been lukewarm Catholics ready to make concessions to outsiders, instead of holding fast to the real doctrines and acknowledging the claims of the Catholic Church. Such persons have altogether ceased to belong to her, and hence they are prone to go forth from our midst (1 John ii, 19); whereas naturally those who antagonize the Catholic faith find it to their purpose to regard such persons as genuine Catholics.

Let there be no misunderstanding about the matter: the object of hostility and hatred is not any alleged erroneous teaching of the Popes nor the asserted cunning of the Jesuits, but it is invariably the Catholic Church, the Church founded by Christ Himself, and her One, Holy, Catholic, and Apostolic doctrine.

Protestants say that in every age there have been among Catholics wise and prudent teachers, and not a few good Christians who put to shame many "evangelical" Christians, with whom they are united in charity since they approximate closely to them in the faith. On the other hand, Catholics dominated by the spirit of the Popes regard Protestants as heretics, that is to say, not as true Christians, worthy only of abhorrence, and this feeling of hostility reveals itself in public life and daily intercourse.

It is true that in every age there have been great saints among Catholics, and men such as St. Benedict, St. Francis of Assisi, St. Charles Borromeo, St. Francis Xavier have never been counted their own by "evangelical" Christians. These great saints were far from professing the doctrines characteristic of Protestantism; they all laboured with unfeigned humility to perfect their own souls; they served God zealously with good works, but they were invariably scrupulously obedient to the Catholic Church.

A Catholic who truly lives and thinks according to the spirit of his Church will never abhor one who professes another faith, nor will he treat such a man as an enemy. He is able to distinguish between the error and the person who errs, just as he can discriminate between culpable and inculpable ignorance. The Church, being the divinely appointed teacher of truth, can under no circumstances whatever accept any other truth than that revealed to her by God. Should she call error truth, she would be false to the words of Christ, to the testimony of the Apostles, and to herself, and when any one *by his own fault* persists obstinately in error she deals with him in accordance with the rules laid down even by Christ and the Apostles (Cf., e.g., Titus iii, 10).

The Catholic Church, far from teaching us to abhor as heretics those who have grown up in inculpable error, bids us love them as brethren; it would be a grievous sin against Christian charity to persecute those who do not agree with us on matters of religion. We will not discuss here the question as to where indeed hostility and hatred prevail against people professing another faith.

Protestants say that there is a great difference between the statements found in ancient ecclesiastical documents or made at the present day by honest Catholics, on the one hand, and the innovations introduced by the papacy into the public worship of the Church on the other. For instance, they maintain that in the decisions of the Council of Trent the doctrine of indulgences and of the merit of good works is not stated nearly so bluntly as in the papal bulls. They admit that the official utterances of the Church contain much that is good and beautiful, though it is intermingled, they say, with erroneous and disastrous teaching. They recognize the presence of this beneficial element particularly in our Catholic catechisms and devotional works.

In reply to this assertion we may say emphatically that the Pope can introduce nothing contrary to faith into the public worship of the Church, and hence there cannot possibly be any discrepancy between the teaching of the Church and the faith of honest Catholics. It is a strange fallacy to suppose that papal bulls may contain a doctrine differing from that taught by the Council of Trent or from that universally accepted and handed down in the Church. No Catholic catechism in any part of the world contains a sentence contrary to a papal bull. In marked contrast to this unity it is known that Protestant catechisms and religious works of every kind agree in their doctrine neither with one another, nor with the teaching of the Reformation, nor with the obvious meaning of Holy Scripture; while Catholics have not a single article of faith that has not at all times been universally accepted and upheld by the Catholic Church. In a "Protestant Protest against the Evangelical Alliance" (*Volkszeitung*, 1899, No. 181) Dr. Max Oberbreyer wrote: "In our camp there are incessant disputes regarding the chief matters of faith. Was not Leo XIII, the great advocate of peace, perfectly right when he contrasted the solid unity of the world-wide Catholic Church with our divisions? Fieldmarshal Moltke, a truly loyal Protestant, declared that the fact that the Catholic Church possessed a supreme head assured her preëminence on account of her certainty regarding dogma. Moltke's inference was that Protestants must eventually return to the Catholic Church, but many Protestants of our day hope to prop up the crumbling ruins of Protestantism by stirring up the masses against Rome. Their efforts will fail, for the violent assaults of Protestant preachers tend to disgust many of their own persuasion and convince them that a church that resorts to vituperation and slander cannot possibly be the true Church of Christ."

The utmost pains are taken by our antagonists to inspire the young with a horror of Rome, to fill them with a blind hatred of the papacy and with contempt for everything Catholic, so that they may never be tempted to make inquiries for themselves and to find out what the Church really is and what are her history and her aims.

Ceremonies

Protestants say that ceremonies constitute the chief part of Catholicism and that in them there is a large admixture of superstition. Such Catholics as are true Christians cannot of course be satisfied with merely external ceremonies, and have recourse therefore to the remains of evangelical truth that still linger in their Church. People of this class happily always exist, and so long as they do not influence the Catholic Church as a whole, the Popes allow them to serve God quietly; indeed, they are often employed in converting the heathen or in winning Protestants over to Catholicism. As soon, however, as they become prominent in the

Catholic Church they meet with persecution, and no pains are spared to induce them to abandon the truth and to make an at least ostensible recantation of their alleged errors. Mournful instances of such a line of action occur in the history of men such as Francis Speira, Fénelon, Noailles, the Jansenists, Sailer, and his followers, Boos, etc.

If the members of the Protestant Church could boast of no other advantage than freedom from the burden laid on conscience, which oppresses the noblest and best Roman Catholics, they would have good reason for thankfulness.

A Protestant might certainly be amazed at the astuteness of Rome and aghast at the action of the Popes, if they used precisely the honest and pious Catholics, "so long as these do not influence the Catholic Church as a whole," to ensnare worthy evangelicals, and submitted these same persons to persecution "as soon as they become prominent in the Church."

Does the Protestant who utters these accusations believe men like Fénelon and Sailer to have been at heart inclined to Protestantism? Let him read Fénelon's *Treatise on the Authority of the Sovereign Pontiff*. Can he imagine Fénelon's submission to the decision condemning one of his works to have been extorted from him by force, when the great bishop himself wrote on the subject: "In what way did I offend those who charge that it costs me a great effort to subject my feeble intellect to the authority of the Holy See"?

What justification is there for the statement that true Christians, anxious for their own salvation, cannot find peace of mind in the doctrines of Catholicism and are forced to have recourse to the remnants of evangelical truth still lingering in the Catholic Church?

Such a statement is an utter misrepresentation of the truth. We are told that some remnants of evangelical truth still linger in the Catholic Church, when in matter of fact all the really evangelical truths retained by non-Catholic sects have been drawn from the Catholic Church, the Church which has neither lost nor obscured any single one of them. If it were otherwise, Christ's own promise that the Holy Ghost should guide His Church into *all* truth would not be fulfilled. Luther discovered neither new nor forgotten truths; he did nothing but deny and abandon much that had been believed and practised in the Church of Christ from the time of the Apostles onward. If the Catholic Church were to vanish out of the world it would leave a gap that nothing else could fill. No one would be then in a position to declare with certainty who Christ was, what the Bible is, or what constitutes grace and sin. It would be impossible to discover the truth amidst the inextricable confusion of opinions put forward by Protestant theologians and preachers. If their opinions and theories, however, were all to vanish, would the world be deprived of any truth?

We are told, further, that ceremonies form the chief part of the Catholic religion and that there is in them a large admixture of superstition. Never have ceremonies been of paramount importance in the Catholic Church. She is, however, wisely aware that her members are human beings made up of body and soul, and that access to the soul is gained through the senses. One cannot draw water without a vessel to hold it, nor can one receive truth unless it is clothed in words, nor grace without a visible sign. Outward forms of some kind or another are indispensable to the mind of man. The Catholic Church has ever aimed at supplying precious vessels to contain her priceless treasures, and for this reason she surrounds her public worship with stately ceremonial intended to lead the minds of her children to appreciate and thankfully accept what is bestowed and symbolized by the outward forms. Ceremonies are the means of raising men's thoughts to God and of bringing down divine graces; they are not an end in themselves. Of course, no Catholic can quiet his conscience with purely external rites; every child learns this in his catechism. The Catholic Church exerts herself to combat any superstition that may become attached to the outward performance of ritual; it is a well-known fact that a tendency to superstition is deeply rooted in the masses and easily spread. Protestantism has surely not succeeded in eliminating it.

Liberty of Conscience

Further, we are told that if Protestants could boast of no other advantage than freedom from the burden laid on the conscience of Catholics, they would have good reason for thankfulness.

Do Protestants really enjoy complete freedom from every constraint of thought? Is a Protestant candidate for confirmation allowed to interpret the Bible in his own way, and may he act in accordance with his opinion? If he is taught to do so he may not, it is true, become a Catholic, but neither will he long continue to be a Protestant or even a Christian. Any one desirous of knowing Luther's views on liberty of conscience should study his works, as also the constitutions of the various evangelical churches. In his *Table Talks* (Latin ed., p. 288) Luther says: "After admonishing a person two or three times, I will denounce him from the pulpit as excommunicate, should he not obey me; so that he may be regarded as a dog, and if he die thus, he may like a dog be buried in a dungheap." In the regulations of an early Protestant sovereign, Duke Christian, severe penalties are imposed upon the excommunicate, no one is permitted to eat or drink with them, they must not be admitted at an inn, they are to be buried in unconsecrated ground, and are to be cursed and damned with all the devils in hell (Zelle ed., p. 91). In other regulations for the evangelical churches there are similar passages regarding the treatment of heretics and notorious sinners (Böhmer, *Jus eccl. Protest.*, 5, 39, § 55). Did not Luther actually exhort his followers "to seize the pope and all the rabble of adherents to his idolatry, and tear out their tongues by the roots, as blasphemers against God," and "to drown all the papal rabble, all the abominable knaves together"? The leaders of the Reformation regarded it as a matter of course that the Catholic Church ought to be completely destroyed and exterminated. Loud in their condemnation of restraints on conscience, they themselves imposed such restraints without scruple.

Döllinger remarks that it is quite a mistake to describe the Reformation as aiming at liberty of conscience; its tendency was in the opposite direction (*Kirche*, p. 68).

Protestants would do well to refrain from asserting that liberty of conscience is found only in their midst, and restraint prevalent in the Catholic Church, but people at the present day like to hear the same things that Luther told the people of his time. "What gave Protestantism its great attraction," writes Döllinger (who is surely an intelligent and impartial witness), "was that its teaching revealed an easier road to heaven. . . ." It was willingly assumed that the people had been deprived of the sweet consolation afforded by the Gospel, in place of which was put the uncomfortable doctrine that they were bound to keep the commandments of God. According to Brenz, a Protestant writer, freedom from the obligation of penance and of fasting was the bait that won the common people over to Protestantism. They were not slow to identify liberty of conscience, and the new religion itself with freedom to disregard all ecclesiastical and moral laws. Luther himself says (*Gal. Brief*, Walch, 3, 1173) that "the Catholic theologians are asses if they maintain that Christ abolished only the ceremonies of the Old Testament and not also the ten commandments."

What is really the constraint imposed upon the conscience of a Catholic? None other but God's own word and commandment, and Christianity consists precisely in the voluntary acceptation by man of a divine revelation, of divine commandments, and of a Church divinely founded for the purpose of bringing men to salvation. Whoever accepts this definition must necessarily regard God's revelations and laws as binding upon his conscience. This is far more obvious than that a soldier, who has of his own accord enlisted in the army, must endure all hardships and restraints of military service. A Catholic knows that in obeying the Church he is obeying God; this is why in Holy Scripture and in the writings of the Fathers, refusal of belief and disobedience to the Church of Christ was regarded as a grievous sin.

Our pious and noble men are not under constraint, for it is an honour and a joy, not a burdensome duty, to obey God's word and His Holy Church. The yoke that we bear is easy and the burden laid upon us is light and sweet. Half-hearted and lukewarm Christians who long for forbidden fruits may indeed be heard to complain, but they belong not to our pious and noble members. These are rather the countless saints of every age, of both sexes, and of all nations; they all at the hour of death rejoiced at having been permitted to live and die as children of the Catholic Church. Read the story of their lives and see if you can discover any feeling of restraint imposed upon their conscience, or of any other feeling than tender love, heartfelt gratitude, and loyal submission to their holy mother, the Church. Read the experiences of those who, after growing up as Protestants, have returned to the bosom of the Church. Did Luther ever feel such happiness after he abandoned her? He tells quite a different story when he relates how his heart quaked, how he could not himself believe what he preached to others (*Eisl. Tischr.*, 76, 415). The last years of his life were disturbed by anxieties, doubts, and by qualms of conscience. We may read in the second volume of Döllinger's *History of the Reformation* what sort of consolation the new religion had for Melanchthon and many others of the early preachers and adherents of Protestantism.

II. HOLY SCRIPTURE

The Protestant Assertion. The Roman Catholic Church teaches erroneous doctrines regarding the Bible, inasmuch as she maintains it to be of itself insufficient to guide us in the way of salvation and that it needs the support of tradition, viz., of ecclesiastical customs, practices, and regulations.

The Catholic Reply. The Catholic Church teaches that the Bible is a collection of books, written under the inspiration of the Holy Spirit, and containing therefore the word of God. Many Protestants have ceased to believe this. It is true that the Catholic Church maintains the Bible to be of itself insufficient to guide us in the way of salvation. Christ however did not order His Apostles to distribute Bibles, but to preach; nor did He bid His followers to read, but *to hear* the word of God (cf. Matth. xxviii, 19; Luke x, 16). When we speak of tradition we do not mean "ecclesiastical customs, practices, and regulations," which are of human origin, but revealed truths, taught orally by the Apostles and handed down from generation to generation.

Moreover, every Protestant who reads the Bible has previously received some oral instruction which serves for his criterion in interpreting what he reads.

The Protestant Assertion. Holy Scripture is enough to guide us in the way of salvation, for "all scripture inspired of God is profitable to teach, to reprove, to correct, to instruct in justice, that the man of God may be perfect, furnished to every good work" (2 Tim. iii, 15–17). On the other hand, the word of God does not refer us to human regulations such as the Catholic traditions, but warns us against them since they lead us astray and are fraught with danger to our souls (Matth. xv, 9; Gal. i, 9).

The Catholic Reply. The Catholic Church fully endorses St. Paul's words to Timothy, but they do not mean that the Bible *alone* will secure the salvation of every individual who reads it. Timothy himself owed his faith in Christ to the Apostle's preaching, not to reading the Old Testament, and the New Testament did not yet exist. In Matth. xv, 9 our Lord is warning the people against the doctrines of the Pharisees, but He refers to the genuine traditions of the Jews in Matth. xxiii, 2. In Gal. i, 9 St. Paul speaks of false teachers, not of the doctrines of the Church and the Apostles; on the contrary, he expressly exhorts the Christians to adhere to the latter. Again, in 2 Thess. ii, 14 he writes: "Therefore, brethren, stand fast, and hold the traditions which you have learned, whether by word or by our epistle." We are not referred to rules laid down by men but solely to God's word; but we value and respect the word of God equally, whether recorded in writing or handed down orally.

Translations of the Bible

The Protestant Assertion. The Roman Catholic Church teaches erroneous doctrines when she maintains that a simple Christian cannot understand Holy Scripture, and therefore may, by reading it, be led into fatal error. For this reason it is considered inexpedient for the laity to read the Bible, and the Popes have frequently prohibited its translation into the vernacular and have condemned and suppressed such translations.

The Catholic Reply. We read in Holy Scripture itself that it is not easily understood. In several instances Christ's disciples failed to understand passages of the Old Testament (cf. Luke xxiv, 25; Acts viii, 27–35), and His own hearers misunderstood what our Lord said (cf. Luke viii, 10; John vi, 61, etc.). Experience shows that the indiscriminate reading of the Bible has caused many people to fall into lamentable errors. The Catholic Church has never taught that it is inexpedient for the laity to read the Bible. She has, however, with great prudence laid down rules for the use of Holy Scripture. No Pope has ever in general terms forbidden it to be translated, but improper translations, likely to foster and spread erroneous doctrines, have from time to time been suppressed. In acting thus the Popes properly protected the word of God against falsification.

The Protestant Assertion. The Protestant Church teaches that Holy Scripture contains all that it is necessary to know and to believe in order to attain salvation, and that it contains this, moreover, in a form intelligible to any reader honestly in search of truth. Therefore, if men are to be able to die a blessed death, it behooves them to read the Bible, to grow in the comprehension of it, to believe it, and to live in accordance with its teaching.

The Catholic Reply. If Holy Scripture dispensed the truth in so obvious a form, it follows that every reader would inevitably discover in it the same truth. This is not the case even with regard to the chief articles of faith. The Catholic Church has always taught that it is most beneficial and expedient for all who have sufficient education and are in the right dispositions to read and meditate upon Holy Scripture, especially the Gospels.

The Protestant Assertion. The Bible is intended for the poor and ignorant as well as for the learned, for "the testimony of the Lord is faithful, giving wisdom to little ones" (Ps. xviii, 8); it is to be read by the young as well as the old, since St. Paul praises Timothy for having from infancy known the Holy Scriptures (2 Tim. iii, 15), and we read in Ps. cxviii, 9: "By what doth a young man correct his way? Even by keeping Thy words."

The Catholic Reply. In the Catholic Church there is for learned and unlearned alike precisely the same faith, the same teaching on morals, and the same reverence for Holy Scripture. Amongst Protestants, however, the Bible is made to yield different standards for learned and unlearned.

In the Psalms the expressions "the word of the Lord" and the "testimony of the Lord" do not refer exclusively to the *written* word, but even if this were the case the passages quoted would mean nothing more than that this word is good and beneficial. The Holy Scriptures which Timothy knew from his infancy must have been the Old Testament. He learnt through oral instruction the references to Christ in the Old Testament.

Many Protestants, especially those teaching the young,

do not believe that the reading of all parts of the Bible is good for children. Catholic children are well instructed in Holy Scripture, as it forms the basis of all their religious teaching.

COMMENTARY

The Catholic Church values and reverences the Bible as a divinely inspired book, whereas modern Protestant scholars regard it as of purely human origin. It is held by them that scientific theologians of the present day are convinced that the Holy Scriptures were not inspired by God, that many classical works of Greek, Roman, and later origin are superior to the Old Testament; that the Bible is full of errors and contradictions, and even in instructing the young it should be emphasized that it is not infallible. Against this view Pope Leo XIII in 1893 proclaimed publicly that God Himself was the original author of the Bible, and that it points out with certainty the way of salvation. Is then the Bible treated nowadays with greater respect by Protestants or by Catholics? In addition to Holy Scripture we accept, of course, oral tradition; this, however, is not a collection of human regulations, but, like the Bible, divinely revealed truth. Without tradition no one would know what properly belongs to Holy Scripture, and it is only when the genuine ecclesiastical tradition is set aside that false human tradition takes its place. For instance, a person who believes St. John's Gospel to be divinely inspired but rejects the books of Machabees, bases his belief not on Holy Scripture, in which there is not a word on the subject, but on Luther; consequently he relies on the word of a human being. St. Peter warned the faithful that in St. Paul's epistles "are certain things hard to be understood, which the unlearned and unstable wrest, as they do also the other scriptures, to their own destruction" (2 Peter iii, 16).

Moreover, a great and saintly scholar such as St. Augustine (*ep.* 119, cap. 21) acknowledges frankly that in Holy Scripture there is more that he cannot understand than what he can comprehend, and he adds that from the earliest times uninstructed and superficial persons have been apt to misinterpret the Bible. It cannot therefore be a book easily understood by every one. Luther himself complained that every sect appropriated the Scriptures and interpreted them according to its own views, so that finally the Bible fell into disrepute, even came to be called an heretical book, because all heresies had arisen from it and all heretics quoted it. (Sermon against turbulent spirits.)

The Canon of the Bible

Protestants assert that, since the Council of Trent, Roman Catholics have had to regard the so-called apocryphal books as being of equal importance with the other books of Holy Scripture. The Protestant Church holds that this is improper, because those books were not included among their sacred writings by the Jews nor by the primitive Christian Church.

In reply we remark:

(*a*) The books in question are not apocryphal, in the sense of spurious, although Luther called them so. These books, viz., Baruch, Tobias, Judith, Wisdom, Ecclesiasticus, Machabees, and portions of Esther and Daniel have come down to us only in Greek and not in Hebrew, but it is known that among the Jews the Greek text was the standard. It was the Greek text that the Apostles themselves used, and this text included these books. It is known, moreover, that in the third century Baruch was read in the synagogues, and in the Talmud Ecclesiasticus is mentioned with the Law and the Prophets. In the second century B.C. these books were universally regarded as canonical.

(*b*) These books were considered sacred by the Christian Church from the very beginning, and no less importance was ascribed to them than to the earlier books of the Bible. An examination of the writings of the Fathers will show that they used and quoted these books no less than the other parts of the Bible; even so early an author as St. Clement of Rome made use of them; they occur in the most ancient translations, such as the Greek Septuagint, which dates from the third century B.C., as well as in the oldest Latin, Syriac, and Armenian versions. The Oriental sects, severed in the first centuries from the unity of the Church, regard these books as canonical. The Council of Hippo (393) and the Council of Carthage (397) included, like the Council of Trent, these books among the Holy Scriptures handed down by the Fathers, and in the year 405 Pope Innocent I officially confirmed this canon. How then can any one assert that these books were put on a level with the rest of Holy Scripture only since the Council of Trent (1545-1563)? Such a statement involves a perversion of facts.

(*c*) No innovation was made at the Council of Trent nor were there any books added to the canon, but the Council proceeded with regard to the Bible as with other matters, and defined the primitive Christian truth plainly and intelligibly as an article of faith. Not only was the Council entitled to do this, but it was imperative for men to know with certainty which books belong to Holy Scripture and therefore contain divinely revealed truth.

(*d*) Luther, on the contrary, had no right to reject any books nor to designate them as apocryphal, i.e., books that have not the authority of Holy Scripture. It was not his privilege to decide regarding the authenticity of the Scriptures, and he might just as well have rejected every other book in the Bible. This is actually what Luther's followers are now doing. Protestant professors of theology, whose duty it is to train young men for the ministry, speak of the book of Genesis as a collection of myths and legends; they regard the prophets as eccentric, or even more or less demented enthusiasts, who thought that by stern denunciation and malediction they could best serve the terrible God of Israel. The books of Chronicles are assumed to have no claim to authenticity; St. Paul is regarded as a prejudiced Jewish theologian whose writings teem with contradictions, whilst St. John's teaching is said by them to border very closely on heresy. In short, the books of the

Bible are treated as purely literary productions, inferior to many classical writings; they are said to be ingenious fabrications, etc., etc. The foregoing are only a few of the opinions expressed by modern Protestant critics who might as well apply to the whole Bible Luther's definition of the so-called apocryphal books, viz., "books, once regarded as forming part of Holy Scripture, but now acknowledged to be full of legends and fables."

The Catholic Church has a claim upon our gratitude not only, but upon that of every pious Protestant who still looks upon the Bible as the word of God and the source of divine truth. Amidst the storms and conflicts of centuries she alone has preserved the whole collection of sacred books, not tolerating the excision of a single book, chapter, or letter.

The Vulgate

Protestants assert that, since the Council of Trent, the Roman Catholic Church has assigned to the Latin translation of the Bible, known as the Vulgate, an importance equal to that of the original text, and in all her public utterances uses it to furnish conclusive evidence in support of her doctrines. So thoroughly is this the case that, where an error occurs in the Vulgate, it must not be corrected in accordance with the original. For instance, in Gen. iii, 15, the Hebrew text reads: "God said unto the serpent . . . I will put enmity between thee and the woman, and between thy seed and her seed, *he* (or *it*) shall bruise thy head"; but the Vulgate runs: "*she* shall crush thy head." Protestants maintain that our theologians avail themselves of this mistranslation to prove that Mary, and not her divine Son, was to destroy the serpent. They recognize the great value of the Vulgate, but say that its numerous mistakes make it necessary for any one wishing to ascertain the truth to go back to the original.

What have Catholics to say on this subject?

(*a*) The name Vulgate means "generally used." This translation was made by St. Jerome during the years 390–405. He took the greatest pains to secure its accuracy and to render the Hebrew and Greek text with the utmost fidelity into Latin. As time went on, this translation was universally adopted as peculiarly excellent.

(*b*) The Council of Trent declared it to be most expedient for Catholics to know which of all the Latin editions then in circulation was to be regarded as the one officially sanctioned. Therefore the Council decided that the ancient Vulgate edition, which had for many centuries been used in the Church, should be accepted as authentic and that no one under any pretext whatever should reject the same.

(*c*) It is therefore incorrect to say that only since the Council of Trent has the Vulgate been recognized as the translation true to the meaning of Holy Scripture.

(*d*) This translation is described as authentic. In legal language this term is applied to a document acknowledged to be genuine and trustworthy, so that when a translation is called authentic we mean that it conveys essentially the same meaning as the original. But, by calling the Vulgate an authentic translation, the Church had no intention of declaring it to be *preferable* to the Greek or Hebrew original texts of Holy Scripture, nor that it was free from all mistakes, nor that it was forbidden to correct such mistakes in conformity with the original text.

(*e*) The Council merely declared the Vulgate to be the best of all existing Latin versions of the Bible, and forbade another Latin translation to be quoted in public dissertations, sermons, or lectures in support of any doctrine affecting faith or morals.

It was very necessary that such a definite rule should be laid down, since between the years 1515 and 1580 there appeared no fewer than 181 Latin translations of the whole Bible or of individual books in it, these versions being more or less inaccurate. The Council said nothing as to the use of the Hebrew and Greek texts, for it was taken for granted as an incontestable fact that these texts were eminently authentic. Evidence in support of this statement is supplied by such men as Vega, Salmeron, and Pallavicini, who were present at the proceedings of the Council. Rugerius, secretary to the Apostolic See, writes as follows: "How could God-fearing men bear to assent, should any one declare that the Hebrew text of Holy Scripture was thenceforth discarded, — that text inspired by the Holy Ghost, written by the prophets, and quoted and expounded by Christ, — that text whence, as from a fountain, all other versions proceed, and from which all are descended?"

Within our own time Pope Leo XIII, in his encyclical *Providentissimus Deus* (Nov., 1893), urged theologians to be zealous in studying the Bible in the languages in which it was originally written.

(*f*) The Council of Trent did not pronounce the Vulgate to be free from all errors, as is proved by the testimony of Pope Marcellus II, who assisted at the Council as Papal Legate, and also by the fact that both Sixtus V and Clement VIII caused several mistakes to be corrected. These mistakes were verbal inaccuracies and did not affect matters of faith or morals. The Church does nor profess to teach languages, but, where truth necessary to salvation is concerned, she decides what is right or wrong.

The idea that mistakes in the Vulgate may not be amended in accordance with the original text is quite erroneous. Verbal or grammatical errors may certainly be corrected, but it has never been shown that the Vulgate diverges from the original on points of importance and matters of faith. We may be sure that no purely human work has ever been more closely examined and sharply criticized than the Vulgate translation.

(*g*) Protestants fancy that they are pointing out an obvious mistranslation when they refer to the passage in Genesis where the promise of a Redeemer is made for the first time. They say that the Hebrew reads the masculine pronoun, whereas St. Jerome, by substituting the feminine, has given Catholic theologians the opportunity of referring the promise to the Virgin Mary.

We acknowledge that the passage is expressed in the Vulgate otherwise than in our printed Hebrew Bibles, but it is uncertain whether the reading of the Hebrew text used by St. Jerome was identical with that which we now possess.

Some scholars regard the identity as very doubtful, and we know that St. Jerome never intentionally mistranslated any part of the Bible. It is quite a mistake to suppose that this divergency from the Hebrew text has in any way affected or obscured the Catholic doctrine regarding our Redeemer and His blessed mother. Every student of theology is informed that there is a discrepancy between the Vulgate rendering and the original, and a statement to this effect will be found in every Catholic commentary on the Bible. Some Catholic scholars accept the masculine pronoun, but nevertheless find in the passage an allusion to the immaculate mother of our Redeemer, whilst, on the other hand, ·Delitzsch and Keil, who are Protestants, admit that the Vulgate rendering is not incompatible with the meaning.

What, we may ask, did St. Jerome intend to express by his translation?

God said to the serpent: "I will put enmity between thee and the woman, and between thy seed and her seed, *he* (or *it*) shall crush thy head." The masculine pronoun refers grammatically to the seed of the woman, not to any definite person, but the Greek translators, whose version is accepted by Jews and Christians alike, made it refer, not to the seed generally but to one person, so that we have here a plain allusion to the promised Redeemer. No one ever found fault with this rendering, as it really expressed the meaning of God's words.

But St. Jerome substituted a feminine pronoun, which must refer, not to the woman's seed but to the woman herself; hence the passage means that God's grace destined woman alone to be the means of bringing the Redeemer into the world, just as she had brought sin into it. In the original we read that *her* seed, not the seed of man, should crush the serpent's head. Now apart from Jesus Christ no one can be termed the seed of a woman, in the Biblical sense. A non-Catholic commentator (Pember, *Die ersten Zeitalter der Erde*) writes: "In this earliest prophecy we find it stated that our Lord was to be born of a virgin," and he continues:

"If our translators had understood this correctly, they would not, in Is. vii, 14 and Matth. i, 23, have departed from the original by writing "*a* virgin" instead of "*the* virgin, shall conceive and bear a Son.""

Therefore Luther's translation of these prophecies of Isaias is in two places wrong in its wording and deeper significance, whereas St. Jerome's conveys a profound suggestion of the primitive Christian belief in the mysterious meaning of this promise, which contains the first allusion to a Redeemer.

(*h*) The passage just discussed is the only one in which Protestants profess to discover an erroneous translation in the Vulgate, and otherwise they attach much importance to it. Teuffel, a renowned scholar (*Römische Literatur*, 3, 433), calls it a masterpiece from the linguistic point of view, and with regard to its meaning and substance it is admitted to be in perfect agreement with revealed truth. Can as much be said for other translations, especially Luther's?

Luther's Translation

Is the Protestant who opens Luther's Bible sure of finding in it the genuine words of Holy Scripture? Döllinger (*Kirche und Kirchen*) says that it teems with mistranslations which seriously affect the meaning, and that in order to gain support for his own doctrines Luther in several instances intentionally altered the words of the Apostles, particularly in St. Paul's epistles. De Wette, a conscientious Protestant, affirms that in the prophetic books and elsewhere in the Old Testament, Luther's translation is so faulty as often to convey no intelligible meaning at all. What was the opinion of it formed by Zwingli, another leader of the Reformation? He writes: "Luther is an abominable twister and shameful distorter of God's word, . . . he scratched out of Holy Scripture all passages contrary to his teaching" (de sacr. 3). For instance, in order to establish his doctrine regarding good works, he inserted the word "alone" in Romans iii, 28, and a modern Protestant writer says that it is absolutely impossible to understand Luther's translation of St. Paul's epistle to the Romans or the first epistle to the Corinthians (Baumgarten, *Predigtproblem*, 1904, p. 24).

Interpretation of the Bible

With regard to expounding Holy Scripture, Protestants declare that while it is the doctrine of the Roman Catholic Church that she alone interprets the Bible aright, no clear statement was made by the Council of Trent as to the particular person who is to give the interpretation. Cardinal Bellarmine comments that the Church, viz., the Pope with a Council, decides what is the true meaning of Holy Scripture, yet the same writer remarks in another passage that infallibility is the prerogative of the Pope alone, not of a Council nor of an assembly of bishops. Hence in the Roman Catholic Church, councils and bishops have frequently been condemned, in proof that power to interpret Scripture infallibly is not connected with their office, so that all ultimately depends upon the Pope's decision. Protestants profess to know that when the Popes have given an interpretation, it often involved such a reprehensible abuse of the Bible that even a Catholic with any regard for the truth is unable to deny this fact.

Let us begin with the last assertion, and say at once that in our opinion it is extremely reprehensible to make an accusation in support of which no evidence can be adduced. It is impossible to point out any actual instance of abuse of Holy Scripture by any Pope engaged in the interpretation of its meaning. Had such a thing ever occurred, Catholics should certainly have heard of it. Let us now consider the assertions that the Council of Trent did not declare clearly who in the Church possesses the power to decide what is the correct interpretation of Scripture, and that the Pope alone exercises the right of interpretation, often in an unjustifiable manner. Protestants imagine that the Popes may expound the Bible just as they please, and that a Catholic is bound to accept their views as infallible. As a matter of fact, there was no need for the Council to discuss the question who in the Church possesses the power to correctly interpret Holy Scripture on points affecting doctrines of

faith and morals, and such were the points under consideration. It could well presume it as generally known that there
was a teaching office in the Catholic Church, and that every
one knew who held it. There is an explicit statement in the
Roman Catechism, compiled upon the conclusion of the
Council at the command of Pope Pius V.: "The Son of God
appointed some to be apostles, others to be prophets, and
others to be shepherds and teachers, who were to make
known the word of life, that we might be no more like children tossed to and fro, and carried about with every wind
of doctrine (Eph. iv, 14), but might be built upon the firm
foundation of the faith into an habitation of God in the
Spirit (Eph. ii, 22). In order however that no one might
regard the word of God as merely the doctrine of men, but
should receive it as the word of Christ (for this it indeed is),
our Redeemer imparted so great a dignity to the teaching
office of the Church, that He said: 'He that heareth you,
heareth me; and he that despiseth you, despiseth me' (Luke
x, 16). These words applied not only to the persons to whom
our Saviour addressed them, but to all their legitimate successors in this teaching office, and He promised to remain
with them all days, even to the consummation of the world
(Matth. xxviii, 20)." (Introduction to the Roman Catechism, §§ 3 and 4.) Thus the legitimate successors of the
Apostles exercise the authority to teach as long as they are
in communion with the supreme Head of the Church.

An individual bishop, a council not in communion with the
Holy See, even a Pope not speaking officially as the chief
teacher of the Church, they all may err. But the teaching
office of the Church has at all times existed, it has maintained the truth of God against erring bishops such as
Cyprian and Fénelon, against councils not in harmony with
the ancient teaching of the Church, such as the Council
of Bâle in 1431, and even against a Pope (Honorius) who
transgressed the true ecclesiastical law by his imprudent
treatment of heretics, although he did not err in a point of
faith. It is a remarkable fact that the adherents of each

heresy acknowledge the Catholic Church to have acted wisely in defending the truth against heretics of an earlier age, although refusing to admit the justice of her attitude towards themselves. Yet the Church has dealt with Luther's doctrines precisely as she dealt with those of Arius and Nestorius. She examines the teachings, whether they be of God, and denounces error as error, because she exists and has received authority from God for that very purpose. In a civil court of justice the judge's duty is to define and apply the law. The code of laws cannot define and apply itself. An individual may read and study the law, but he must not decide his own case in accordance with his individual conception of it. It is obvious to every one that it cannot be otherwise, and we are all aware that certain men are appointed to be judges, that they sit in courts and give sentence independently of the opinions of contestants. Furthermore, there is a supreme court from whose decision no further appeal can be made, and every subject of the state has to submit to this court even if he previously believed it permissible to differ with the judge of the lower court. Yet Protestants refuse to recognize a similar arrangement in the Church of God, the greatest institution on earth, and the one possessing the loftiest aims. They maintain that there should be no supreme teaching authority, one able to decide disputed points by irrevocable decrees. Had it not existed, what would in course of time have become of the truths taught by Christ? All of them would have perished, or would at least have lost every claim to recognition. It is absolutely necessary that there be a teaching authority in the Church, not simply regarded as competent to decide every question concerning the interpretation of the word of God but really so empowered by Him to speak with infallible accuracy and continually under His guidance. When this teaching authority or its highest representative, the Holy Father, decides what interpretation is to be given to Holy Scripture, it does not claim to be superior to the word of God, no more than the judge claims to be superior to the law, but it is above the private opinions of the faithful, no matter how pious and learned they may be, and it is in a position to detect and condemn any error that might otherwise find acceptance.

When we reflect that the organic Church dates from Pentecost, and that portions of the Bible were not written until a hundred years later, is it an exaggeration to assert — indeed, were it not rank fallacy to disown the fact — that the Church of the New Law antedates the authorship of the New Testament? And this being accepted, is she not the "author and mother," and therefore (aside from divine appointment) the interpreter, of the work of her own children?

Dr. Philip M. Rhinelander, Bishop of the Episcopal Diocese of Pennsylvania, said exactly this in a lecture delivered July 8, 1911, in Cambridge, Mass., and quoted by the *Boston Republic*. "It is the Roman Catholic view and treatment of the Bible that has been vindicated at every point by the often excessively anti-Catholic examination of the student"; and because of this "leading critics have finally come to the opinion that since the Bible comes from the Church, it must be restored to the Church — for proper interpretation, of course — in order that it may be understood."

In order to prove the Catholic Church incapable of interpreting Holy Scripture, Protestants say: "If the Council of Trent made the interpretation of the Bible dependent upon the agreement of the Fathers, it is equivalent to an admission that the Fathers of the Church are not always in accord." They refer in this connection to Professor Möhler's book on the dogmatic differences between Catholics and Protestants.

A reader who has not Möhler's book nor the decisions of the Council at hand, might suppose the Council of Trent to have laid it down as an absolute rule that Holy Scripture must be interpreted in accordance with the unanimous teaching of the Fathers, and that Möhler has shown that they are never unanimous. If this were true, the Catholic would indeed be in a bad fix. But if we examine the two books in question we find that the Council of Trent forbids any one, relying upon his own knowledge, to interpret Holy Scripture *on any point of faith or morals* in accordance with his own views, as opposed to the meaning assigned and accepted by our holy mother, the Church, or opposed to the unanimous testimony of the Fathers. It is quite plain that here, too, the Council is referring only to interpretations of Holy Scripture which affect *the faith and morals* of Christians, and Möhler himself states that all Fathers of the Church agree on these points, and could not do otherwise. He writes: "Apart from the interpretation of a few classical passages, it would be difficult to say on what subjects they are all agreed, except that they all derive from the Bible *the same doctrines on faith and morals*, although each does so after his own fashion, and thus some have produced works that are for all time models of what exegetics should be, others are men of merely average capacity, whilst in the case of others, their good will and their love of our Saviour constitute their only claim to our veneration." In another passage Möhler foresees that in the future similar comment will apply to Catholic writers on Holy Scripture, "but, like the Fathers of the Church, they will all discover in the Bible *the same dogmas and the same moral teaching*" (2d ed., § 36).

The Fathers are absolutely unanimous as to the Catholic faith. If we studied all the hundreds of volumes in the Patrology we should find that they all held the same belief and bore testimony to it. All declare Jesus Christ to be really the Son of God, true God and true Man. Mary is His virgin Mother, the Mother of God, and consequently entitled to our veneration. Jesus founded a visible Church, gave to her a visible Head, made her the infallible teacher of revealed truth, and required all who would be saved to belong to her body. These are articles of faith upon which absolute unanimity prevails among the Fathers, a unanimity so striking that it alone has caused many non-Catholics to return to the true faith. The fact that the patristic writers do not agree on other, minor, points shows that Catholics are at liberty to examine and interpret Holy Scripture without restriction, always provided they do not question the teaching of the Church on matters of faith and morals, and even here the faith of the Church and the tradition of the Fathers are trustworthy guides rather than impediments. Every one needs some guide in reading the Bible, for should he discover in it another faith than that taught by Christ, preached by the Apostles, held by the Fathers and defended by the blood of martyrs, it would not be the true faith by which alone he can be saved.

(*i*) It is absolutely false and misleading to say:

"We know that the Son of God nowhere bestowed on any body of men or any individual sole authority to interpret the Bible."

We know that the Church must have power to teach and that from the time of the Apostles this teaching office has existed in the Catholic Church, having been instituted by Christ who made her a stronghold of truth, resting on St. Peter as on an immovable rock. Moreover, He gave the Apostles authority to teach, and the power to interpret the Bible is included in this authority. We are convinced that if the Church had not possessed this teaching office divine truth and Holy Scripture would long ago have perished, since Satan himself may be numbered amongst the exponents of the Bible (Matth. iv, 6).

"We must confess that there are scores of preachers now in Protestant pulpits conceitedly dealing out destructive criticism and cunningly undermining the faith of the people, who would be promptly silenced by Catholic authority. How strange the times and how humiliating to our reformed profession!" (Rev. E. P. Marvin, in the *Episcopal Recorder.*)

Individual Interpretation

Protestants attempt to prove from the Bible the doctrine that every Christian ought to find out his faith by searching the Scriptures. They maintain that Christ said to every one, "Search the scriptures" (John v, 39), and that the Apostles would have approved had any man, after hearing them preach, examined the Old Testament to see if their doctrine

33

were in accordance with it (Acts xvii, 11). They say, further, that the words of Christ and His Apostles and prophets give light unto the simple and are "living and effectual, . . . reaching unto the division of the soul and the spirit" (Hebr. iv, 12).

With regard to the words: "Search the scriptures," a Protestant, the learned Seldon, remarked that they have had a disastrous effect upon the world. If Christ addressed them to His disciples, did He mean that every man, woman, and child ought to read and interpret the Bible? If we examine the passage in which they occur, and consider their context in St. John's Gospel, we shall see that our Lord did not address these words even to His disciples, far less to all men universally as some Protestants allege, but only to the unbelieving Pharisees. It was to them that He said: "You search the scriptures, for you think in them to have life everlasting; and the same are they that give testimony of me; and you will not come to me, that you may have life." Our Lord's meaning was that the Pharisees searched the Scriptures, but had formed from them an idea of the Messias totally unlike the picture of the real Redeemer as foreshadowed in the Old Testament. Being misled by this mistaken idea, derived erroneously from the Scriptures, they failed to recognize Christ as their Redeemer, and did not attain to everlasting life through Him, because they assumed to have found it in the Holy Scriptures alone. Unhappily there are many people at the present day who make the same mistake.

Our Lord recognizes the importance of the Old Testament Scriptures which give testimony of Him, but He points out that a misunderstanding of them leads neither to Him nor to life eternal. In uttering these words He certainly had no intention of bidding every one read the Bible.

Such is the interpretation given by the best commentators, both Catholic (see Schanz, *Joh.-Evangelium*, p. 257) and Protestant (see Stage, *Neues Testament ad loc.*). It is important to notice the concluding words of our Lord's address to the Pharisees: "Think not that I will accuse you to the Father. There is one that accuseth you, Moses, in whom you trust. For if you did believe Moses, you would perhaps believe me also, for he wrote of me. But if you do not believe his writings, how will you believe my words?" The Church that He founded, and in which He, the Son of God, lives on even to the end of the world, might well use the same language towards her antagonists. She might say: "Think not that I will accuse you to the Father — your accusers are the prophets and apostles. If you believed them you would believe me also, for they wrote of me. But if you do not believe their writings how will you believe me?"

A further mistaken assertion is that the Apostles would have commended their hearers, had they referred to the Scriptures in order to test the accuracy of their doctrine. We read in Acts xvii, 11, that certain Jews in Berea received the word with all eagerness, daily searching the Scriptures whether these things were so. It does not, however, follow that Christian believers were bound to do the same. St. Paul was preaching to unbelievers, quoting the prophecies relating to a Redeemer, and the Jews referred to the Old Testament to verify his quotations. It was not through searching the Scriptures, but by listening to the Apostles' words that they received the faith. When St. Paul was addressing Christian congregations, and not Jews, he never suggested their examining written documents to see if he was teaching true doctrines, but he confirmed the churches, commanding them to keep the precepts of the Apostles, and delivered to them the decrees that were decreed by the Apostles and ancients at Jerusalem; and the churches were confirmed in faith (Acts xv, 41; xvi, 4, 5).

As to the words of Holy Scripture being a light to enlighten the simple-minded, the Catholic Church is far from denying that this is the case, but neither in Hebr. iv, 12 nor in other similar passages does she discover any recommendation of indiscriminate Bible reading.

Some Protestants are willing to admit that there have been misinterpretations of Holy Scripture, but they believe that God has raised up men in every age capable of giving the correct interpretation, men like Martin Luther, Wesley, etc.

If Protestants admit that there are many erroneous interpretations of Holy Scripture, how are they to know which is the correct interpretation? Do they not realize that it is impossible for more than one interpretation of a given passage to be true and correct?

At the Last Supper our Saviour said: "This is my Body." After uttering these words, what He held in His hands was either truly His Body or it was not; and if it was not, Christ did not mean what He said. Only one of these alternatives can be true, and in reading the Gospel you are perhaps undecided as to which is correct. You are liable to error, and many of your predecessors, men perhaps even more earnest than you in the quest of truth, *have* erred, in spite of possessing the Bible.

Your Protestant friends bid you search the Scriptures, and tell you they alone can reveal the right path to follow, but in your own heart you feel that you are in a state of danger and uncertainty, and likely to go astray; in fact these friends add to your difficulties by their admission that it is possible to err in the interpretation of the Bible. In your perplexity you feel the need of authoritative interpretation. But where are you to go for the truth? Must you have recourse to exponents such as Martin Luther, Wycliffe, or Wesley? No, these are individuals quite as liable to make mistakes as you yourself, and it is admitted even by their disciples that they have often blundered. If you, for instance, asked Harnack or any other modern Protestant scholar for his opinion of Luther's interpretation of the Bible, you would not be edified by their reply. You would be still more amazed to learn of all the mistakes and contradictions into which Luther fell.

Nevertheless let us see what Luther holds as to what our Lord did at the Last Supper. In his earlier works he says

36

quite bluntly that you must not believe the bread to have been changed into the Body of Christ, but later he taught a very extraordinary doctrine, viz., that Christ did not actually change the bread but gave to the Apostles His Body in and with the bread. Later still, Luther found a way out and pointed out that Christ as man is everywhere present, therefore He is present in the Sacrament, and hence He can say: "This is my Body."

If none of these interpretations satisfy you, you may be referred for others to the writings of other Protestant commentators, but whichever you choose to adopt, it is the explanation given by some human individual and not simply the statement found in Holy Scripture. Where then can you find certainty regarding the word of God?

Since it is universally granted that individuals may err in interpreting the Bible, must not our Lord necessarily have entrusted His Word to some infallible authority, able to recognize, maintain, and teach with certainty the true meaning? Is it not in fact an inestimable benefit that He did so? Considered merely from the human point of view,. the Catholic Church, with her uninterrupted tradition and her unchanging deposit of faith, is far more trustworthy an exponent than Luther or any other individual commentator, since they explain the Bible in accordance with their own opinions. We Catholics should indeed be both blind and ungrateful, if we failed to appreciate the great advantage that we enjoy.

The Right to Read the Bible

Protestants are fond of declaring that since the thirteenth century the Popes have discouraged and forbidden the study of Holy Scripture, and they mention Pius IV, Sixtus V, Urban VIII, and Pius VII especially as having done so. The papacy, we are told, wishes Christians not to read the Bible and to have as little access to it as possible, so that they may retain the belief in papal doctrines. Protestants say they owe much gratitude to God, and should implore Him to preserve to them and their posterity that greatest of privileges, the right to read the Bible.

(*a*) Is it recorded anywhere in Holy Scripture that the right to read the Bible is the greatest privilege enjoyed by Christians? "Master," said the rich young man, "what must I do to be saved?" Was he told to read the Bible? "Which is the first commandment in the law?" asked the Pharisees. Was the reply "Read the Bible"? In the Sermon on the Mount our Lord taught His disciples the new law; did He say, "Blessed are those that read the Bible"? When He founded His Church did He say that the Scriptures were the rock? Did He charge the Apostles to go forth into all the world and distribute Bibles? Is there in the Bible itself a word as to the necessity of reading it? No, Holy Scripture does not say anything at all on the subject.

(*b*) For centuries, in fact ever since the time of Luther, Protestants have stuck to the zealously promulgated fable that the Popes are sworn enemies of the Bible, and have forbidden Catholics under heavy penalties to read it. This accusation is quite groundless; no Pope has ever feared the Bible nor forbidden its use in the Catholic Church. It is quite clear from historical records that in the primitive Church people were encouraged to read the Scriptures; even Protestants do not question this fact. But, some one may ask, why did not the early Christians, our forefathers in the faith, or the learned doctors filled with the Holy Spirit, or the heroic martyrs who died rather than surrender their holy books to their persecutors, find in the Bible some of the things that Luther discovered? Because they possessed greater humility, and did not presume to set themselves up as judges of the word of God, but recognized the Church founded by Christ as alone competent to interpret the Scriptures. They were of the same mind as St. Augustine who said, "I should not believe the Gospel, unless the authority of the Catholic Church impelled me to do so" (*Ep. fund.*, c. 5), and, "Let any one, who fears to be misled by the obscurity of Holy Scripture, have recourse to the Church, which is pointed out to him in the Scriptures" (*c. Crescon.*

Donat., I, 33, 39). No one ever knew and loved the Bible better than St. Jerome who made it universally accessible by his translations and elucidations, and yet he writes (*ad Paulin.*, c. 7) that "every garrulous woman, every puerile old man, every busybody, recklessly meddle with Holy Scripture and presume to teach others before they themselves have learnt." He goes on to complain that some scholars completely misinterpreted Holy Scripture according to their own ideas, adding that it is exceedingly wrong to distort the sense when it is at variance with one's own opinions. This goes to show that already in St. Jerome's time individuals were not allowed to read and interpret the Bible as they chose, although Protestants claim this to have been the case, so that they may represent the subsequent action of the Holy See as an encroachment upon the rights of Christians.

(*c*) Why did the Popes forbid certain translations of the Bible to be circulated and read? In order to protect the Bible against falsification and Christianity against error, Pius IV laid down the following rule: "Since experience has shown that, if the use of the Holy Bible in the vernacular be allowed to every one without distinction, there results therefrom, in consequence of the rashness of men, more harm than advantage, let all submit in this matter to the judgment of their spiritual superiors, who have the right to allow the reading of the sacred scriptures, translated into the vernacular by Catholics, to such as will derive from this reading no injury of any kind, but an increase of faith and piety."

Whenever the Catholic Church deems it expedient to assign certain limitations to the reading of translations of the Bible, she fears, not for herself, but for ignorant readers. If the Popes had really wished to conceal the truth from Christians in general, they would have done better to forbid scholars to read the Bible in Hebrew or Greek, since the truth would be more certainly discovered in the original text than in a translation. But no restrictions have ever been imposed upon reading the Bible in the original languages.

In course of time, the free practice of Bible reading became a token of rebellion against the ancient Church, especially among the Waldensians and Albigenses. Men began to find all sorts of doctrines in the Bible. The Anabaptists, for instance, discovered that every imaginable form of licentiousness could be justified from the Bible. Such grave disorders compelled the Catholic Church to take stringent measures for their repression.

The Bible in the Middle Ages

It is a common tale, accepted by most Protestants as incontestably true, that in the Catholic Church the Bible was despised and neglected until Luther restored it to honour.

To this fairy tale the *Living Church* (Episcopal) editorially replies: "Luther did not discover the Word of God to the Germans, despite the Protestant delusion to that effect. Those who have cared to learn have long ago known that many editions of the Bible were published in Germany in German and Latin before Luther's time."

"Before the time of Luther the Bible had already been translated and printed in both High and Low Dutch" (Menzel's *History of Germany*).

As a matter of fact, Catholics have never neglected the Bible nor do they disregard it at the present day. No one who has ever read a mediaeval book or sermon can possibly imagine that in the Middle Ages people despised and ignored the word of God. As long ago as 1861, a writer in a Protestant newspaper said: "In the darkness of the Middle Ages, when a Bible cost as many pounds as it now costs pence, unfamiliarity with the Bible and inability to answer religious questions were not as widespread as they are among the present generation." During the Middle Ages the Bible was translated into many languages and was widely circulated. In 1294 a complete French translation was made, but single books of Holy Scripture had long before this date been translated and circulated among the faithful. Before the time of Luther there were in existence two hundred translations into the vernacular, and between the invention of printing and Luther's first appearance at least twenty translations of the Bible into German were printed. The fact that the Reformation was contemporaneous with the invention of the printing press has given Protestants the opportunity to claim the credit for the increased output of Bibles in the vernacular, which was really the immediate and direct result of the invention of printing. Between 1471 and 1500 seventeen editions of an Italian Bible appeared, and in 1538 there was another revised edition of it, besides many others. In every case these Bibles were sanctioned by the Church, which permitted them to be printed, published, and circulated. Surely no one can suppose that there would have been so many editions had people been forbidden to read the Bible!

Even Adolf Harnack admits to be false the assertion "that Catholicism forbids laymen to read the Bible." Emphatically he adds (and in italics): "On the contrary, Catholicism has at all times undoubtedly regarded Bible reading as useful and salutary for every man in the abstract, and is still of the same opinion" (*Bible Reading in the Early Church*).

To-day, when there are "nearly seven hundred sects in England alone, each of them proving a whole system of theology and morals from the Bible" (*London Times*, May 13, 1884), and when "the Bible and the Bible alone" is the rule of faith of many earnest religious people, is it not embarrassing for them to remember that for many centuries this salvation-through-the-Bible was generally impossible? Impossible because, although as we have seen, the people were encouraged to read them, it cannot be expected that every home was provided with copies of the sacred writings in an age when trained and patient hands were obliged to transcribe the inspired words to parchment rolls.

How do matters stand at the present day? Do Protestants really believe Catholics to be unaware that the Bible contains the word of God, or to be deprived of any truth recorded in

Holy Scripture? Every Catholic child is required to learn the catechism and Bible history, both derived from and based upon Holy Scripture. The Council of Trent advocated the study and interpretation of the Scriptures, and the Popes recommend accurate translations. It was with the full consent of Leo XIII that in 1900 a society was established in Rome for the purpose of circulating among the people a correct translation of the New Testament at a very low price. On November 29, 1903, Pius X addressed words of commendation and encouragement to the members of this society, laying stress upon the fact that the reading of the Gospel was a safeguard of the faith.

In the Catholic Church Holy Scripture has at all times been treated with reverence as the word of God. Saints knelt when they read it, and every Catholic can study it without let or hindrance, provided he does so for the purpose of edification and with a pure intention. He must, however, assure himself that the book before him is really the word of God, correctly translated and expounded as it has been in the Church from the time of the Apostles onward. This assurance is supplied by the approbation of a Catholic bishop, which is the only condition the Popes now insist upon.

By putting wise and necessary restrictions upon the reading of translations of the Bible, the Church shows her respect not only but even her jealous care for Holy Scripture. A Catholic who does not believe Holy Scripture to have been revealed by God, who does not believe that its teaching, rightly understood and expounded, will bring him to God, errs on a point of faith, and, whether he be priest or layman, if he persists in this error or attempts to propagate it, he will be excluded from the Church.

Protestant Opinion of the Bible

What, however, do many Protestants of the present day think of the Bible? Father Ignatius, an Anglican, expressed the most profound admiration for Leo XIII's encyclical on the Study of Holy Scripture, and described as a magnificent act of faith the Pope's assertion that the Bible, being inspired by the Holy Spirit, was free from all error. He pointed out also that Protestants of every variety depreciate the Bible and do their best to undermine all faith in it, whilst the Roman Pontiff comes forward as its champion, offering consolation to those who are oppressed with sorrow at the conflicting doctrines taught in the world (Catholic Times, 1893).

(*d*) Protestants appear to take peculiar offence at the vigorous opposition of the Popes to the so-called Bible Societies.

It should be borne in mind that a Bible Society is not the same thing as the Bible, nor did Christ say to the members of such societies, "He that despiseth you, despiseth me." One may disapprove of abuses in the butter trade and yet appreciate good butter; he will be anxious to protect it against adulteration. In the same way, one may have the greatest admiration for the Bible and yet oppose certain actions of Bible Societies. A well-known Protestant (Professor Leo) remarks on this subject: "The Pope calls the Bible Society a pest, and he is right. If I were in his place, I should do the same, for the Bible is but the sheep's skin under which the wolf is concealed." Other prominent Protestants have spoken in similar terms of these societies (cf. Perrone, *de loc. theol.*, p. 2, c. 4, § 277).

The first Bible Society was founded in London in 1804, its aim being to exercise an apostolate by circulating the Bible amongst pagans, Mahommedans, and Christians. It is obviously impossible to spread the Gospel amongst the heathen by merely distributing Bibles (Rom. x, 14), and it was surely the duty of the Popes to emphatically forbid utterly unauthorized men to carry on amongst Catholics a proselytizing for Protestantism under the pretext of giving them the Gospel, which in truth they possessed from the earliest age. Moreover, the emissaries of these Bible Societies publicly declared that they aimed at overthrowing the authority of the Popes and at converting Catholics, and they distributed not only Protestant Bibles, but tracts full of vehement attacks upon Catholic faith, and containing misrepresentations and calumnies of the Catholic Church.

Oral Traditions

Protestants maintain that Roman Catholics are bound to accept, as on a level with Holy Scripture, all sorts of oral traditions said to date from the time of the Apostles and to have been preserved in all their purity. Most of these traditions are rejected by Protestants, as not only manifestly opposed to the word of God but also because for the most part they originated some centuries after the death of the Apostles.

The two objections against oral traditions require proof before they can be given any weight. The Council of Trent declares explicitly that no traditions are to be accepted, believed, and respected except such as the Apostles received from the lips of Christ and such as were handed down by the Apostles under the inspiration of the Holy Spirit. These traditions alone must not be rejected.

Catholic traditions regarding the Mass, Purgatory, papal supremacy, etc., are not opposed to Holy Scripture. On the contrary, they are all based upon the word of God and by no means repugnant to it. If non-Catholics tell us that they can find no allusion to these things in their Bibles, this proves nothing except that Holy Scripture by itself does not teach all doctrines clearly and beyond misinterpretation. If two people assign different interpretations to a legal enactment, they must have recourse to some higher authority to settle the matter. We Catholics have such a supreme authority to decide the true meaning of Holy Scripture and of oral tradition, viz., our Holy Church, in which Christ lives on in accordance with His promise: "I am with you all days, even to the consummation of the world." He cannot fail to guide her into all truth.

It is certain that our divine Lord Himself employed no other means but oral instruction of making His doctrines known. He bequeathed not a single word in writing to His followers, and yet He entrusted all His words and teaching to His Church to be her inalienable possession. It is certain, moreover, that He charged the Apostles to teach, not to write (Matth. xxviii, 18; Luke x, 16). It is certain, too, that the Holy Scriptures are not so ancient as the oral tradition of the truth, and that the Apostles, even when some special purpose caused them to write, nevertheless regarded oral instruction as the means designed by God for the propagation of the faith, and they impressed upon their converts the importance of adhering to the doctrines they had been taught orally. Both in ancient and modern times, heathen nations have received the faith and have clung to it loyally, although it reached them solely through the channel of Apostolic tradition. Finally, it is certain that the Fathers of the Church always appealed to the tradition, handed down pure and undefiled from one generation to another, just as it was given in the first instance, by Christ to the Apostles, and they appealed to it successfully against heretical teachers. Catholics have not allowed human ordinances to make their way into the deposit of faith received from the Apostles; their living and universal consciousness of the faith would have rendered this impossible, and Christ's promise of guidance by the Holy Ghost would have failed. Those, however, who rank human wisdom higher than the word of God, those who have cut themselves off from the unity of the old faith, are the Protestants. The Holy Scriptures with their inexhaustible wealth of doctrine belong to the Catholic Church. She was entrusted with them and she has been true to the trust. Ever since Protestants claimed the Bible as their own, it has by them been misinterpreted, mutilated, and dishonoured. We Catholics are the heirs of the Apostles who, like their divine Master, taught their followers to hold fast to the truth, warning them at the same time against false prophets, against newfangled doctrines, and schism. Hence we, the same as our forefathers, adhere to the word of God, which will be handed down in our Church, in Holy Scripture, and in the ancient traditions to the end of the world, for our Lord said: "Heaven and earth shall pass away, but my words shall not pass away."

III. THE CHURCH AND ECCLESIASTICAL AUTHORITY

The Protestant Assertion. According to Catholic doctrine the only true Church, the Church in which alone salvation can be found, is the visible community of Christians under the rule of the Roman Pontiff. Every member of this Church must make outward profession of the faith that she teaches and conform to her ordinances.

The Catholic Reply. We read in Holy Scripture that Christ founded a visible Church and commanded men to obey her (John xx, 21; Matth. xxviii, 18, etc.). Moreover, we read that He Himself appointed one man to be the visible head of this one visible Church (Matth. xvi, 18, etc.; John xxi, 15–17). Hence it is true that we believe the Church of Christ to be the visible community of all the faithful, who recognize the Roman Pontiff as the supreme head of the Church appointed by Christ.

The Church does not teach that a merely outward membership of her body is sufficient to ensure salvation. A merely outward member of the Church would resemble a lifeless limb on a living body. Nor does she say that all who are not outwardly her members are therefore excluded from salvation. Many are in error through no fault of their own; they serve God to the best of their knowledge and inwardly belong to His Church; hence they can be saved.

The Protestant Assertion. The true Church consists of the invisible communion existing between all who believe in Christ, no matter what outward form of religion they profess.

The Catholic Reply. The theory of an invisible Church is opposed to the plain statements made by Christ and the Apostles. In Holy Scripture the Church is always said to be visible as well as invisible. St. Paul, for instance, frequently

46

speaks of the Church as the body of Christ. Just as Christ performed His work of redemption in a visible body, so will He continue the work in a visible Church to the end of the world.

It is not a matter of indifference which religion a man professes, for not every religious body supplies to its members the means of receiving the true faith and of living a life pleasing to God.

Protestants maintain that they possess the Gospel of Jesus Christ in all its purity and the sacraments as He instituted them.

The Catholic Reply. It is impossible that the various existing religious bodies that call themselves Churches should all equally proceed from Christ and lead men to Him. Protestants seem to describe their Church, which they allege to be that which Christ founded, sometimes as visible, sometimes as invisible; surely there is some discrepancy here! It is, moreover, false to assert that in the Protestant Churches the Gospel of Christ is preached in all its purity, and the sacraments administered according to our Lord's institution. The name of "Protestant" is given to all those who have cut themselves off from the one holy Church of Christ, although they may agree on no other point except their severance from the Catholic Church. If we rely upon the statements made by Protestants, we may venture to say that never has the Gospel of our divine Lord and Saviour Jesus Christ been so corrupted, never have the sacraments been so neglected and reduced in number, as by the various Protestant sects at the present time. The Catholic Church, on the contrary, can adduce historical evidence to prove that she alone has faithfully preserved the Gospel of Christ in its integrity as she received it, and that she has always administered the seven sacraments according to our Saviour's desires.

Authority of the Pope

Protestants assert that Catholics give the following account of the authority of the Church: Supreme and unlimited power over the Church is in the hands of the Pope, the successor of Peter the Apostle and Vicar of Christ. But the Pope possesses authority also over the whole world, and every human being is subject to this authority and unless he acknowledges it he need not hope for salvation. Hence in matters of faith and morals the Pope is infallible, and what he teaches and orders must be believed and carried out with absolute fidelity. He has power to release men from their vows, to appoint and depose kings, to distribute the countries of the world according to his wishes, and to coerce unbelievers and heretics by the agency of secular governments or even to order their extirpation.

The Catholic Reply. We believe and confess that Christ Himself (Matth. xvi, 18) conferred upon St. Peter the privilege of acting as His representative in governing His Church, and as this office is essential to the continued existence of the Church the privilege must pass on to the legitimate successors of St. Peter.

Further, we believe that the supreme teaching office in the Church, the pillar and ground of the truth (1 Tim. iii, 15) must be infallible (Luke xxii, 31, etc.).

We are only then absolutely bound to believe and do what the Pope teaches and orders when he acts in his capacity as the chief shepherd and teacher of the Church and gives a decision, applicable to the whole Church, on a matter which is imperatively necessary for us to believe or obey in order to be saved.

On the other hand, the Pope claims not a positive privilege of temporal power, far less a dominion over the entire world. Christ said: "Preach the Gospel to every creature; he that believeth and is baptized, shall be saved, but he that believeth not, shall be condemned" (Mark xvi, 15, 16). Hence our Lord desires all who wish to be saved to submit to the teaching authority of the Church, but it is a silly calumny to say that for this reason Catholics ascribe to the Popes the power to assign the countries of the world, to depose kings, etc. False assertions of this kind are made only in order to inspire ignorant Protestants with hatred and horror of Catholicism, and especially of the Holy Father. "The Roman See has never taught that Catholics are not bound to keep their word in dealing with non-Catholics, nor that it is lawful to break an oath taken to non-Catholic monarchs, nor that the Pope may interfere with the rights and property of secular rulers" (Cardinal Antonelli).

The Protestant Church, on the contrary, teaches that Jesus Christ is the sole Head of His Church and needs no one to act as His representative, since He will abide with His followers in word and spirit, in His sacraments and graces, even to the end of the world. He appointed ministers to preach the doctrines taught by the Apostles and prophets and to edify both themselves and their congregations by means of the Gospel, and these ministers are entitled to control the outward discipline of the Church. But they have no right to appoint or depose kings, to exercise secular power, to release men from their oaths, to stir up riots, or to persecute those of another faith with fire and sword.

The Catholic Reply. Whether or no the Church requires any one to act as the representative of Christ, is a matter for Christ and not for us to decide. He is, of course, the one supreme, invisible Head of the Church and will abide with her unto the end. It was in order to accomplish this design that He appointed a visible ministry (John xx, 21; Matth. xxviii, 19), whose office is not, however, only to preach, as Luther imagined, but to be the teachers, priests, and shepherds of all Catholics, and our priesthood can be traced back in an unbroken line to the Apostles.

We are quite ready to admit that Protestant ministers have no power of government nor have they any right to persecute men of another faith; but why have they, nevertheless, on many occasions shown great cruelty and intolerance towards those who do not agree with them, and why do they still continue to malign and slander the Catholics?

COMMENTARY

It is quite certain that one religion is not as good as another, and it is of the utmost importance for us to be sure that we belong to the one Church founded by Christ.

1. Christ founded only *one* Church whereby all men might be saved; cf. John x, 16: "There shall be one fold and one shepherd;" Matth. xvi, 18: "Upon this rock I will build

my church;" Ephes. iv, 4–6: "One body and one spirit . . . one Lord, one faith, one baptism: One God and Father of all." St. Cyprian (died 258) says: "There is one God, one Christ, one Church, and one See, founded by the word of the Lord upon the rock."

2. Our Holy Catholic Church can make the following statements about herself and the testimony of Christianity in all ages will vouch for their truth: —

"I am the only teacher of truth appointed by God; I am the only steward of His divine gifts of grace, and the only safe guide to eternal life, for (*a*) I am *one*, since everywhere I teach the same doctrine, administer the same sacraments, and acknowledge the same supreme Head. If contemporaries of Luther, of St. Augustine, and of the Apostles, respectively, could now come forward, they would recognize my doctrine as the word of God, my seven sacraments as true channels of grace, my supreme Head as the lawful successor of Peter, and me myself as the same mother who watched over their childhood.

(*b*) "I am *holy*, for my Founder is holy, and it is my task to lead all my children to Him, the Holy One. I have never taught error nor falsified the means of salvation. Innumerable saints in every age have been my sons and daughters.

(*c*) "I am *Catholic*, intended for men in every age, of every nation, and of every rank. There has never been a time when I was unknown, nor a nation to which I was not sent.

(*d*) "I am *Apostolic*, carrying on from age to age the light of truth kindled by Christ and conveyed to me through the Apostles. I keep pure and unadulterate the stream of graces that flows from the foot of the Cross."

3. Just before His ascension our Lord said briefly and emphatically, "He that believeth not shall be condemned" (Mark xvi, 16; cf. John iii, 18, 36). He founded *one* Church and said of her, "If a man will not hear the Church, let him be to thee as the heathen and publican" (Matth. xviii, 17), and gave her authority to bind and to loose on earth and in heaven (Matth. xviii, 18). The Catholic Church knows

and can prove herself to be this one Church founded by Christ, hence she can never admit that her Lord and Master has any bride except herself since she alone is holy and without blemish (cf. Ephes. v, 25–27). Her children have always been firmly convinced of the truth expressed by St. Cyprian when he says, "No man can have God as his Father, who has not the Church as his mother" (*de unit. eccl.*, c. 6), and "Outside the Church there is no salvation." When therefore the Catholic Church claims that in her alone salvation is to be found, she is acting in conformity with our Lord's words and is no more to be accused of presumption than is our Lord for speaking of Himself as the Son of God.

Since salvation is to be found in the Catholic Church alone, she invites all to enter her fold in accordance with her Master's command, but she condemns none who without their fault do not outwardly belong to her. If any one *obstinately* cuts himself off from her communion and renounces her doctrines he ceases to walk in the way of life, and even St. John, who insists so much on the duty of charity, forbids his disciples to receive such a person into their houses or to salute him (John ii, 10). Any one, however, who acts according to the dictates of his own conscience and errs through no fault of his own may be saved. But he may be saved, not by his adhering to false doctrines by which the truth is obscured but rather because he possesses some remains of the one ancient Catholic truth, for such remnants of the faith are preserved even by the Christians separated from the Catholic Church, and resemble an inheritance carried by a wanderer away from his home into foreign countries.

Origin of the Papacy

With regard to the papacy, Protestants acknowledge that the early bishops of Rome were highly respected, but they deny that in the primitive Church Rome occupied the position that she now does, of mother and mistress (*magistra*) of all other churches.

In reply it may be pointed out that unity in faith and communion cannot exist unless there is a visible centre and a common ruler. Wherever in the world men unite for any common purpose there must be a centre of unity. Even in the Protestant national churches there is a governing body, but in their case it cannot claim any divine origin and commission. Where was in the early ages of the Catholic Church this indispensable centre of unity, without which she would inevitably have perished during the centuries of persecution or have succumbed to the attacks of heretics? Whither did men turn in search of the supreme arbiter, whose utterances upheld the truth? It is impossible to discover in the writings of the Fathers or in those of any other early author, whether friend or foe, a single allusion to any centre of unity except Rome, or to any head of the Christian Church except the Pope, the Bishop of Rome.

Even if no direct statement to this effect existed it would not be reasonable to assume that it was otherwise. But we have evidence enough to show that the early Christians regarded the Roman Church as their mother and mistress precisely as we do to-day. Even Professor Harnack, a famous Protestant theologian, admits that in the first three centuries the bishops of Rome possessed an unmistakable primacy of jurisdiction over the whole Church (*Dogmengesch.*, I, p. 404, etc.).

St. Ignatius, a disciple of the Apostles, calls the Church of Rome the "president of the bond of charity," i.e., of Christendom; a dispute at Corinth was settled by St. Clement, the Bishop of Rome, even during the lifetime of St. John the Evangelist; St. Irenaeus tells us that every church is bound to agree with the Roman Church on account of her preëminent position; St. Cyprian calls the Roman Church "the mother," and says that he who forsakes the See of Peter must not imagine himself to belong to the Church, since the Roman See occupies the first place. In short, the whole of ancient Christianity is permeated by the idea expressed by St. Ambrose in the words, *Ubi Petrus, ibi ecclesia*, "wherever Peter is, there is the Church."

Protestants maintain, however, that the supremacy of Rome was long in question, that finally only a few isolated communities in other countries professed allegiance to the Roman bishop; it was not until the emperors became Christians that the supremacy of the bishops of Rome was universally recognized. Gregory the Great declared, about the year 600, that whoever arrogated to himself the title of "universal bishop" was a forerunner of Antichrist, and therefore he could not have regarded himself as having unlimited spiritual jurisdiction over Christendom. _

No evidence is forthcoming in support of the assertion that the churches of Christendom submitted to the Bishop of Rome only at a later stage. What motive could they have had for thus voluntarily submitting to him if they had not from the beginning regarded him as their lawful superior? Experience shows that individuals and communities are far more apt to seek independence than to become subject to a common head. The writings of the early Fathers abound in admonitions to those disposed to sever themselves from Catholic unity, and they lay great stress upon the necessity of union with the Church and the Bishop of Rome. Even heretics in every age have desired union with Rome; for instance, in the year 160 Marcion, a Gnostic, appealed to the Pope. If once the Bishop of Rome solemnly declared that any man had fallen away from the faith of the Apostles and the ancient Church, that person was no longer regarded as a true Christian by any Christian community in the world. Thus, in the second century, Pope Hyginus excommunicated Cerdo and Valentine as heretics. After teachers of heresy had tried in vain to win over the Popes to their way of thinking, they invariably displayed utmost hostility to Rome.

It certainly did not occcur to the Roman Pontiffs to exalt themselves above the whole of Christendom, but they, like all the faithful from the Apostolic age onward, were perfectly aware that in accordance with the will of Christ they were called to occupy the highest position in His Church of which they were the visible head. They did not arrogate this honour to themselves but received it from Christ. It is foolish to assert, in spite of all evidence to the contrary, that only after the lapse of six centuries all the bishops began to regard the Bishop of Rome as their spiritual head, that even Gregory the Great was unaware of any special prerogative belonging to the Popes! Gregory recognized most fully his position as supreme head of the Church, and was energetic in enforcing its recognition by others. He would not allow John the Faster, the bishop of Constantinople, to assume the title of oecumenical or Catholic patriarch because it might give rise to misunderstandings, and he declared emphatically that the Pope had the right to call himself the universal or Catholic bishop; and while the Popes had not used this title, it had been conferred upon them by the Council of Chalcedon. The bishop of Constantinople openly and repeatedly acknowledged his see to be subject to that of Rome (Greg., *M. epist.*, l. ix, cp. 12, *ad Joannem Syrac. episc*).

The Primacy of St. Peter

Protestants maintain that a change took place soon after the time of Gregory the Great and that then the Bishop of Rome became the Pope, basing his claim to supremacy upon the fact that our Lord founded His Church on St. Peter. But the other Apostles received the same powers as St. Peter (Matth. xviii, 18), and he even allowed himself to be corrected by St. Paul. According to many Protestants St. Peter was never Bishop of Rome and therefore the Popes cannot pretend to be his successors; yet it was owing to this fiction that the papacy acquired the vast power it possessed under Gregory VII, Innocent III, and Boniface VIII, and to this day the Popes uphold the same claim.

"A change took place soon after the time of Gregory the Great." How was this possible? Our opponents suppose that the Church could without a visible head emerge triumphant from the centuries of greatest inward and outward conflict, and then suddenly all Christendom consented to acknowledge voluntarily the supremacy of the Bishop of Rome, without a protest on the part of any other bishop, without question as to Rome's right to take precedence. Such a thing is inconceivable; the rock must always have been there, otherwise in the early centuries of Christianity the gates of hell would many times have prevailed against the

Church, and the same rock stood firm in the Middle Ages as it does to-day. Each successive generation clung closely to it, but fresh foes devised fresh modes of attack, necessitating recourse in many cases to fresh methods of defence.

It is quite a mistake to imagine that it occurred to the bishops of Rome, after the time of Gregory the Great, to base upon our Lord's words to St. Peter (Matth. xvi. 18, 19) a claim to be entitled to govern the whole Church. Such a claim would have been rejected with scorn, had it not always existed from the time of the Apostles onward and had it not been universally recognized as justified by our Lord's commands. At the present time many thoughtful Protestants admit the truth of this argument. For instance, Schelling (*Phil. der Offenb.*, II, 301) says: "Christ's words decide once for all the foremost position occupied by Peter among the Apostles; nothing short of the blindness induced by party spirit could make any one fail to perceive this fact."

That the other Apostles also possessed great powers we Catholics know perfectly well, and we reverence these powers, which are still enjoyed by our bishops and which Christ undoubtedly intended to continue in His Church. But did the other Apostles possess all the authority bestowed upon Peter? No; to him alone were addressed the words, "Thou art Peter, and upon this rock I will build my Church," to last not for one generation only, but as long as the gates of hell assail it; "I will give to thee the keys of the Kingdom of heaven"; "Feed my lambs, feed my sheep."

What do Protestants think is proved by the fact that St. Paul withstood St. Peter to his face (Gal. ii, 11)? We must understand first why he did so. He blamed St. Peter for yielding to the prejudices of Jewish converts, as also St. James and others had done. Any one else was free to act as he chose in such a matter, but Peter, on account of his exalted position, was bound to set an example and not to mislead others, and therefore St. Paul rebuked him whereas he did not remonstrate with St. James. Even at the present day every bishop, and in some circumstances every Catholic, has a right to put forward his own well-grounded opinion in opposition to that of the Holy Father and to offer resistance to any manifest injustice on his part. Such is the teaching of Bellarmine, one of the most ardent supporters of papal authority (*de Rom. Pont.*, II, 29). St. Paul was not singular in availing himself of this right, and his example has been followed by many great saints such as St. Bernard, St. Catharine of Siena, and St. Bridget, whose action in this respect has been no obstacle to their canonization, nor did St. Paul's rebuke at Antioch cause any breach between him and St. Peter or prejudice the reverence paid to the latter in the Church.

Some Protestants declare that St. Peter was never Bishop of Rome, and that therefore the Popes cannot claim to be his successors. This is an extraordinary statement. If it is correct, who then was the first Pope and where did he come from? Did he suddenly take possession of a see that did not exist, exercise an office that had never been instituted? Even though the title of "Pope" was not given to St. Peter and his immediate successors, he was regarded by the early Church in precisely the same way as we to-day regard Benedict XV, i.e., as the visible head of the Church appointed by Christ. All of St. Peter's successors have been recognized as such, and although individually they discharged the duties of their office in various ways adapted to the circumstances of the age and the needs of the Church, they were all convinced that they were appointed by Christ to guide and govern the Church as His representatives, and all Christians in communion with them knew in every age that where Peter is, there is the Church founded upon the rock (Jerome, *ep.* 15 *et* 16).

A Protestant scholar writes as follows: "If the prince of the Apostles ever set foot in the eternal city, he certainly came not as an ordinary traveller but in virtue of his Apostolic power, and his martyrdom was but the glorious conclusion of the active work done in accordance with his calling amongst the people of Rome. Further, if episcopacy is of divine institution — and many Protestants believe it to be so — the claim of the Roman Church to trace back the line of her bishops to the Apostle Peter does not appear unreasonable" (Lipsius, *Zeitschrift für prot. Theol.*, 1876, p. 562).

It is both true and untrue to say that the claims put forward by Gregory VII, Innocent III, and Boniface VIII are still made by the Popes of the present day. It is quite correct and obvious to every thoughtful person that the present Pope claims the rights inseparable from the government of the Church throughout the world just as every previous Pope has done. If he acted otherwise, he would not be discharging the functions of his office.

Papal Jurisdiction and Influence

It is, however, a mistake to include amongst these rights claimed by the Popes now, all the jurisdiction in secular matters ever held or claimed by any Pope. In the Middle Ages the Pope was acknowledged by common consent to be the greatest benefactor of nations and the defender of civil and national rights and liberty. Hence the then existing international law conferred upon him very far-reaching powers in civil matters, and when these powers were exercised wisely and vigorously the nations submitted voluntarily to the Pope's orders, in which they saw no illegal oppression but rather beneficent measures for their defence. These powers, however, were not directly connected with the government of the Church, and they have been withdrawn as Pope Pius IX publicly declared in 1871, so that the Popes now no longer either possess or claim them. It is foolish to alarm people by speaking of the extraordinary powers of interference in civil life which the Pope is said to claim. Under the energetic and imposing rule of Popes like Gregory VII, Innocent III, and Boniface VIII the papacy was outwardly mighty, but these men aimed at promoting only the highest interests of mankind, not at enslaving nations or the human intellect. They desired to secure the triumph of truth and the liberty of nations and to protect the Church against arrogant princes. They wished the Church of Christ to be free and to protect her, so that in accordance with her divine commission she might lead all men along the surest way to everlasting salvation.

Böhmer, the renowned historian, remarks that in the Middle Ages the Pope was not at all what unhappily many writers assume him to have been, viz., a monster enthroned in St. Peter's at Rome, ready to hurl into the abyss any living creature that would not slavishly cringe before him.

Not one but many volumes would have to be written if all the misrepresentations, distortions, and falsifications, intentional and unintentional, of Catholic doctrine and historical facts were to be corrected. Many books have indeed been written on this subject, but they are useless as long as people wilfully close their ears to the truth. Some calumnies and misrepresentations never fail to bob up again no matter how often they have been proved false.

It seems more profitable to make regarding the papacy a few statements that are acknowledged to be historically true, although Protestants seldom hear these things, so great is their fear of the subject.

Herder, who was by no means particularly well disposed towards the Catholic Church and the papacy, was forced by the study of history to confess that the Pope might justly exclaim to every age: "But for me, you would not be as advanced as you are." This is literally true.

Dr. Robert Ellis Thompson, a Presbyterian minister and head of the Central High School in Philadelphia, said recently: "The Protestant historians are coming more and more to recognize the splendid services the Papacy rendered to Christendom in rescuing the Church of Christ from the slavish dependence upon the civil power which is seen in the Greek communion, and especially in Russia.

"Thus on foundation laid by the great Popes was built that independence of the Church from civil control which is the basis of American religious liberty."

To whom does the whole of Christendom owe the faith and the high standard of morals and education that is the outcome of that faith? The first of all missionaries was the first Pope on the first Pentecost, and his immediate successors sealed their testimony to Christ with their blood. They resisted, with equal steadfastness, the persecutions that assailed them from without and the terrible force of false doctrines that would have destroyed the spirit of Christ within the Church. Even from the beginning they showed themselves to be the rock of truth, and but for them all morality and faith, all Christ's words and works would have inevitably perished and left no trace on earth. Sometimes Christian rulers have allied themselves with teachers of heresy and threatened the Church with violence, using ambitious but faithless prelates to further their designs and to interfere with the government of the Church. The Popes invariably withstood this danger, and at the cost of terrible struggles they upheld the liberty of the Church and at the same time vigorously defended the freedom of nations. Non-Catholic writers, if they are impartial in their judgments, acknowledge how much we now owe to the great Popes of the Middle Ages. Herder, for instance, says: "It was through the Pope that England, as well as the greater part of Germany, and the Kingdoms of the North, Poland, and Hungary, became Christian countries. It was due to him that Europe was not overrun permanently by Huns, Saracens, Tartars, Turks, and Mongolians. But for the Roman hierarchy, Europe would probably have fallen a prey to despots; it would have been the scene of incessant warfare, unless indeed the Mongolians had reduced it to a desert." Von Müller asks, "What would have become of us without the Popes?" and supplies the answer, "We should have fared like the Turks."

Dr. Kip (Rev. Wm. Ingraham Kip, D.D., later Bishop of the Episcopal Church in California) frankly and sorrowfully admits that it is, indeed, in a spirit of prejudice "that those outside her fold are accustomed to estimate everything which relates to the Church of Rome. They look at her course through the Middle Ages, and denounce it all as one long period of evil and darkness. And yet, at that time, the

Church — changed as she may have been from her early purity — was the only antagonist of the ignorance and vice, which characterized the feudal system. It was a conflict of mental with physical power, and by the victory she gained, the world was rescued from a debasing despotism, the triumph of which would have plunged our race into hopeless slavery. . . . No one, indeed, can read the writers of the 'Ages' which we call 'Dark,' without feeling that beneath the surface was a depth of devotion, and a degree of intellectual light, for which they have never received due credit" (*Christmas Holydays in Rome*, p. 282).

Only those who are blinded by ignorance and prejudice can fail to see that the Popes not only faithfully guarded the priceless treasure of faith and were unwearied in their efforts to make it more widely known, but they also preserved morality, civilization, and culture against all the assaults of enemies, and bestowed these gifts upon the nations of Europe. "Education for all" were the words uttered by Innocent III ages before they became the war cry of the foes of Holy Church and of the people. The Popes desired all to receive education and did their utmost to put it within reach of the labourer as well as the king's son, for as another Pope, Alexander III, declared, we ought not to sell for money a gift bestowed on us by heaven, but offer it gratis to all.

There have never been more vigorous and resolute supporters of liberty than the Popes. Gregory I, Eugenius IV, Sixtus IV, Pius II, Innocent VIII, and others issued orders for the suppression of slavery. Paul III, Urban VIII, Benedict XIV, Pius VII, and Gregory XVI advocated the setting free of negro slaves and upheld the rights of the Indians and other pagan nations. As recently as May 5, 1888, Leo XIII declared that the abolition of slavery in Brazil had been the gift most welcome to him on the occasion of his jubilee as a priest.

In the Pope, Christian nations have always found their most efficient and often their only protector against violence and injustice. Those who reproach the Popes for having

60

dared to oppose secular rulers are most ungrateful as well as unreasonable. That the Popes ventured to act as they did is most honourable to them. What would have become of Church and state if the Popes had been cowardly enough to raise no protest against unjust deeds on the parts of kings and princes and had been content to flatter them? They stood like St. John before Herod and withstood the mighty of this world, saying when occasion arose, "It is not lawful." In their dealings with all men they used the language of truth and justice and boldly reminded kings and emperors of their sacred obligations towards God and their subjects, whilst at the same time the papacy gave powerful support to secular government. The Popes never failed to insist upon the principle, "Fear God, honour the king," enunciated by St. Peter, the first occupant of the See of Rome (1 Peter ii, 17). As St. Augustine says of the Church, they taught kings to care for their people and admonished the people to obey their kings (*de moribus Eccl. cath.*, I, 30). They added to the title of king the beautiful words "by the grace of God." Whenever the secular power begins to be contemptuous of support, it is on the verge of its downfall. This view is expressed by Proudhon, a modern revolutionary, who writes as follows of the much maligned Boniface VIII: "The kings went so far as to lay violent hands upon the Pope. They believed that they no longer needed any support except that afforded by the sword and the justice of their cause. From that time onward the monarchy tended to decline, for when the Church was disregarded the principle of authority was shaken to its foundations. Thenceforth every citizen could defy the king and say: 'Who are you, that I should obey you?'" (*Confessions d'un révolutionnaire.*)

The Papacy and Civilization

The nations of the present day boast of their knowledge of truth, of their civilization and orderly life, but the light in which they walk would not illumine their way had it not been kindled at that sacred fire brought down by Christ from heaven, — that fire which no one on earth has so faithfully maintained and watched over as the Roman Pontiffs, although they are frequently ignored and actually despised as hostile to the light. The papacy is still with us, imposing in its dignity in spite of all hatred and opposition and although it has in every age been assailed with all the violence and diabolical cunning which men could devise. No name is so frequently mentioned in every language spoken in the world as that of the Holy Father, and though he has no army to enforce his commands and extend his dominion, there is no one whose utterances are received so reverently and obeyed so loyally, or for whom so many thousands of hearts feel such intense love and veneration.

Where is the chief stronghold of the truths of Christianity which afforded strength and consolation to our forefathers in every generation? Every one acquainted with the tendencies of the age must acknowledge it to be in Rome. Hardly any one outside the Catholic Church now ventures to speak of religious topics as if perfectly convinced of their truth. In these sad times there is no positive faith in Christ as indeed the Son of God and our only Saviour, no faith in the efficacy of His death on the Cross or in the imperative duty to follow His example, no faith in freedom of will or purity of heart except in the Church of which the Roman Pontiff is the supreme teacher and pastor.

If we consider all these facts, and observe how the papacy has outlasted the greatest empires and survived the most furious onsets, we are forced to ask how this could possibly be if it were really founded upon a system of deception.

The very existence of the papacy is the best evidence of its divine institution. The unworthiness of an occupant of the Holy See has not been permitted to frustrate God's design in establishing this supreme office or to diminish the value of the treasures intrusted to his charge. At the Council of Ephesus not a protest was raised when Philip the legate proclaimed what has invariably been the faith of the Catholic

Church: "It is a fact, recognized in every century, that St. Peter, the Prince and chief of the Apostles, the pillar of the faith and foundation stone of the Catholic Church, received the keys of the kingdom of heaven, and in the person of his successors still lives and governs."

Lord Macaulay says of the Papacy:

"There is not, and there never was, on this earth, a work of human policy so well deserving of examination as the Roman Catholic Church. The history of that Church joins together the two great ages of human civilization. No other institution is left standing which carries the mind back to the times when the smoke of sacrifice rose from the Pantheon, and when camelopards and tigers bounded in the Flavian amphitheater. The proudest royal houses are but of yesterday, when compared with the line of the Supreme Pontiffs. That line we trace back in an unbroken series, from the Pope who crowned Napoleon in the nineteenth century, to the Pope who crowned Pepin in the eighth; and far beyond the time of Pepin the august dynasty extends, till it is lost in the twilight of fable. The republic of Venice came next in antiquity. But the republic of Venice was modern when compared with the Papacy; and the republic of Venice is gone, and the Papacy remains. The Papacy remains, not in decay, not a mere antique; but full of life and youthful vigor. The Catholic Church is still sending forth to the furthest ends of the world missionaries as zealous as those who landed in Kent with Augustin; and still confronting hostile kings with the same spirit with which she confronted Attila. The number of her children is greater than in any former age. Her acquisitions in the New World have more than compensated her for what she has lost in the Old. Her spiritual ascendency extends over the vast countries which lie between the plains of the Missouri and Cape Horn — countries which, a century hence, may not improbably contain a population as large as that which now inhabits Europe. The members of her community are certainly not fewer than a hundred and fifty millions; and it will be difficult to show that all the other

Christian sects united amount to a hundred and twenty millions [census of 1840]. Nor do we see any sign which indicates that the term of her long dominion is approaching. She saw the commencement of all the governments and of all the ecclesiastical establishments that now exist in the world; and we feel no assurance that she is not destined to see the end of them all. She was great and respected before the Saxon had set foot on Britain — before the Frank had passed the Rhine — when Grecian eloquence still flourished at Antioch — when idols were still worshiped in the temple of Mecca. And she may still exist in undiminished vigor when some traveler from New Zealand shall, in the midst of a vast solitude, take his stand on a broken arch of London Bridge to sketch the ruins of S. Paul's" (*Miscellanies*).

The Papacy and Civil Government

Protestants assert that the civil government has often come into conflict with the papacy in consequence of the demands made by the Popes.

No one denies that the Jewish and Roman authorities often opposed Christ and His Apostles, and that our Lord more than once foretold to His disciples that they would be dragged before kings and rulers for His name's sake. We should be justified, therefore, in viewing with distrust any form of church government that in all respects had invariably been in complete accord with the secular power.

Of sovereigns excommunicated in the Middle Ages by the Popes, we hear much of the German emperors, Henry IV and Frederick II; the former aroused universal indignation by oppressing his people, and incurred the sentence of excommunication because he bestowed bishoprics on his own favourites or sold them to the highest bidders. He even presumed to order Pope Gregory VII to relinquish his see. The princes and bishops of Germany fully approved of the Pope's action, and finally, in order to save his throne, Henry came as a penitent to Canossa and was there released from the ban laid upon him. He was not, however, forced by the Pope to come, but rather did so in opposition to the Holy Father's desire. Even Protestant historians admit that Gregory VII had the right on his side. Gregorovius, an historian hostile to the papacy, calls the incident at Canossa the triumph of moral force over savage despotism and acknowledges that the monarchy was degraded, not by the Pope but by the emperor.

Frederick II was excommunicated because with the help of Saracen princes he plundered churches and monasteries, appropriated the possessions of the Church, made no secret of his unbelief, and failed to keep the solemn oath by which he had pledged himself to go on a Crusade. Under certain circumstances it was taken for granted that the Popes had power to depose as well as to excommunicate secular rulers; this involved no usurpation of power, but was recognized by secular governments as a right belonging to the papacy.

The Papacy and the Church

Protestants assert that the pretensions of the papacy have led to disputes with general councils, bishops, and scholars, and in corroboration of this statement they refer to the condemnation of the Councils of Constance and Bâle.

The Council of Bâle was not a general council, nor was that of Constance, when the sessions were held in which the relation of the council to the Pope was under discussion. These are historical facts. Even in the primitive Church there were divisions and heresies, so it need arouse no surprise if subsequently also bishops, both individually and in councils, as well as Catholic scholars came into conflict with the Popes. It does not follow, however, that in so doing they necessarily had the right on their side.

Protestants tell us that the utterances of the Popes are enough to reveal the true character of the papacy, and they quote the following and similar passages: "We declare, assert, and decide that all creatures are subject to the Roman Pontiff, and without this belief none need hope for salvation." "The Roman Pontiff is the vicegerent of God and Christ on earth. He possesses plenitude of power over all nations and states, he can judge every man, but has no judge superior to himself."

It seems unreasonable to quote detached sentences, written at a time when opinions prevailed such as we are unable now to appreciate. Would it not be more sensible to refer to the encyclicals of a Pope like Leo XIII, who discussed the relation between the spiritual and temporal power? Protestants suppose that it makes no difference whence they take their quotations, since the Popes have abandoned none of their pretensions and Benedict XV would now claim the same rights as Boniface VIII. This is certainly true as far as the essential rights of the papacy are concerned, for no Pope can relinquish any of the prerogatives attached by Christ to his office. He must guard what has been transmitted to him, otherwise he would be unfaithful to his sacred duties and to the Church of Christ. But in their attitude towards the civil government the Popes must adapt themselves to the age in which they live. It would be foolish to suggest that the Popes of the first three centuries assumed the same position towards the Roman emperors as was assumed by those of the Middle Ages towards the German emperors. It is no less foolish to try to make people believe that the utterances of a mediaeval Pope against the secular government of his day are applicable to the present time.

As a matter of fact, however, the words of Boniface VII convey just what St. Cyprian, St. Augustine, and St. Jerome had taught long before, and what was a legitimate deduction from our Lord's words spoken when He instituted the office of chief bishop (Matth. xvi, 18), viz., that the only sure way to salvation was in the Church founded by Himself on the rock of Peter. If the Pope judges any man he does so only with regard to things belonging to his office, such as faith, unbelief, virtue, or sin; and he never judges arbitrarily but in accordance with the unchanging laws of God. There must be a supreme judge and it is his duty to act thus, and the greater his power the greater is his responsibility. His official verdicts cannot be criticized by any higher authority on earth, but the whole Church witnesses his actions and knows what powers her supreme head is authorized to use.

Papal Infallibility

Protestants are fond of discussing the dogma of papal infallibility, proclaimed by the Vatican Council in spite of the opposition offered by many eminent and learned bishops. They maintain that according to this dogma the Pope can alter the rules laid down by Christ and the Apostles and introduce new doctrines unknown to the early Church. He has a right to control all the discipline, worship, and ceremonies of the Church; he can utter and revoke sentence of excommunication; he can lay nations under an interdict and release them from it. He claims the right to appoint all bishops and has power to remove them; he calls general councils, presides over them, and confirms or repudiates their proceedings; moreover, it is within his prerogative to demand contributions from the property of the Church. Everything, both great and small, in the Church is subject to his supervision.

The Vatican Council did nothing more than declare to be a dogma of faith something which had been held without question by our forefathers. The infallibility of the supreme teacher appointed by Christ, on matters affecting faith and morals, is only a logical result of the foundation of the one Church for the purpose of affording all men a sure way of salvation. If the truth revealed by God was not to perish, if the food of souls was to be imparted and the right way of life taught to all men, there must be some one able to decide with infallible certainty what Christ taught and wished. Our Lord's aim was that all men might be saved, hence He must desire means to exist for the realization of this aim; in other words He must intend that there be one infallible teacher in His Church. It was for this reason that He prayed (Luke xxii, 31, 32) that St. Peter's faith might never fail and bade him, being once converted, confirm his brethren. Döllinger interprets this commission according to Catholic doctrine, and says: "The See of Peter was to be a stronghold of truth, a bulwark of firm faith for the support of all, for our Lord's words and prayer did not apply merely to one individual at one particular moment, but to the whole Church and its future needs; they both laid the foundation and built upon it. Looking forward over all future ages, Christ prayed in similar fashion for the unity of all members of His Church, in order that this unity should ever bear eloquent testimony before the whole world to the truth of His divine mission."

Reasonable men perceive that there must be some one centre of unity in the Church and that this can be preserved only by means of an infallible teaching authority. Thus E. von Hartmann says: "Papal infallibility is the long-desired culmination of the unity of faith in the Catholic Church, and all argument to the contrary is unmeaning on the lips of those who regard the Pope as the successor of Peter, and Peter as the author of infallibly inspired epistles."

Even Luther recognized the need of an infallible supreme teacher of truth, and decided that he would himself occupy this position. He says: "There is no angel in heaven, still less is there a man on earth, capable and bold enough to criticize my doctrine. He who refuses to accept it, cannot be saved, and he who thinks otherwise is destined for hell" (*Works*, Wittenberg ed., II, Erlang., 28, 144). Luther certainly owed it to his followers to bring forward some proof of his right to use such language, whereas the infallibility of the Pope rests upon the same immovable foundation as the Church herself.

Protestants tell us that many eminent and learned bishops opposed the definition of papal infallibility as a dogma of faith; no doubt they would have considered these bishops still more eminent and learned if they had persisted in their opposition after the definition was promulgated. Protestants perhaps are not aware that before every session of a council the Holy Ghost is invoked and begged to assist the members in discovering and stating all the obstacles to the definition of a dogma. Therefore it is not only permissible but obligatory for the assembled bishops to state their difficulties. Yet one of them, the Bishop of Cuença in Spain, who was universally acknowledged to be a very learned man, was not contradicted by any one when he said, amidst general applause, that the objections raised to the definition were put forward by persons who were far from refusing to accept the doctrine of infallibility, but wished to elicit the grounds for it in order that the truth might be more clearly revealed. Therefore every one was perfectly free to say what he liked against the definition, and nevertheless it was unanimously declared to be a divinely revealed truth. From the merely human point of view we can hardly imagine a better guarantee for its accuracy. It is a manifest distortion of the truth on the part of Protestants to declare that the Pope alters the law of Christ and the Apostles and introduces newfangled doctrines unknown to our forefathers. The Vatican Council made the following explicit statement on this subject (sess. 4, cap. 4): "In accordance with the circumstances of the time, the Roman Pontiffs have always propounded for our belief those doctrines which they, by God's aid, recognized as in harmony with Holy Scripture and the tradition of the Apostles. For the Holy Ghost was promised to St. Peter's successors not in order that they by His revelation should make known a new doctrine, but in order that by His assistance they should carefully preserve and faithfully interpret the revealed truth handed down by the Apostles, i.e., the deposit of faith." The gift of infallibility is bestowed upon the Pope that he may safeguard the teaching of Christ and the Apostles, and allow no new doctrines to find their way into the ancient faith handed down to us by the early Church; it is most assuredly not intended to enable him to introduce doctrines that he himself has devised.

To a Catholic it seems childish to enumerate the powers exercised by the Pope. All his authority is due to the position that he occupies in the Church. It would lead us too far from the subject to discuss in detail the ecclesiastical points to which allusion is made; moreover, what can it matter to a Protestant, who cares nothing about the Pope, whether he regulates the breviary or the ritual of the Church or claims a share in her possessions? Every Protestant may rest assured that the Pope's demands are moderate in comparison with those of some secular governments.

The Powers of the Pope

The Pope is alleged by Protestants to claim the following powers as his rights: Supreme dominion over every individual soul, exercised by means of indulgences and anathemas (the latter terrible word is supposed to mean abandoning the soul to hell and Satan); power to determine the lot of the dead. We are told that the Pope ordered the angels to bear to Paradise the souls of such as died on pilgrimage to Rome, that he is constantly calling souls out of purgatory, and that we are bound to recognize and invoke as saints all whom the Pope declares to be such. This is supposed to be the power of the keys, ascribed to the Pope, and we are asked where in Holy Scripture we can discover that the Son of God instituted such a papacy, bestowed upon it such authority, and made us subject to it.

No, such statements are not to be found in Holy Scripture, nor are we told that we are to be subject to a papacy of this sort nor that our salvation is assured. All that we find is that Christ instituted the office of supreme teacher, priest, and shepherd, and bade us submit to it if we wish to be saved. The Bible contains nothing at all on the subject of the Protestant Churches and their systems of government. Not only is it impossible to discover in Holy Scripture any trace of such a papacy as the Protestants describe, but it is equally impossible to discover such a thing in any Catholic Catechism or in the mind of any Catholic. Christ did indeed most solemnly and without restriction give the keys of the kingdom of heaven to St. Peter (Matth. xvi, 19), but when the state intrusts to the governor the keys of a prison, no one supposes that he can imprison and release men as he chooses. When a sovereign gives the keys of the treasury to an official, is it that he may use the money as he likes? Certainly not. In every case the person holding the keys is bound to use them in accordance with the wishes and orders of the owner who intrusted him with them, and the Pope can exercise his authority only in accordance with the wishes and instructions of Christ. No Catholic is ignorant of this fact. The Pope cannot close the gate of heaven against any one who desires to be saved and honestly does what God requires of him, nor can he open that gate to any obstinate and impenitent sinner. The Pope cannot command any angel to bear to Paradise the soul of one who has died in the state of mortal sin even though he was on a pilgrimage to Rome, nor can he hand over to the devil the soul of one who has died in the state of grace. Nor is he able to release souls from purgatory and to raise to the altars as saints men whom God has not sanctified. No Pope has ever claimed to possess such powers.

The question of indulgences will be discussed later. As to anathemas, St. Paul pronounced an anathema against every preacher of heresy (Gal. i, 9), and even speaks of delivering a notorious sinner in Corinth over to Satan (1 Cor. v, 5). When the Pope pronounces sentence of excommunication he solemnly declares that the person concerned is cut off from the communion of the Church and her means of grace, but he by no means condemns him to eternal perdition. He tells the excommunicated person that he is not on the road leading to life everlasting, and this is necessary in order that the faithful may be put on their guard. It is not the Pope who hands over an obstinate heretic or an impenitent sinner to Satan, but the heretic or sinner himself by his heresy or sins which separate him from the truth and grace of Christ. No Pope has ever uttered a sentence of eternal damnation against any man, whereas it is a notorious fact that Luther cursed the Pope, the bishop, and all who did not agree with him. For instance, he addressed Schwenkfeld thus: "May the Lord curse thee, thou Satan, and may thy spirit, that calleth thee, and the way that thou runnest, and all who have dealings with thee, be damned with thee and thy blasphemies" (*Table Talk*, 74, 6).

If ever a Pope has prayed that angels might carry to heaven the souls of those who died on a pilgrimage to Rome, and if he happens to use words that might convey the idea that he calls upon the angels to do so — though I know of no such utterance — every Catholic understands that the Pope has neither the wish nor the authority to command angels to carry direct to Paradise a soul that is still contaminated with grievous sin. Should a pilgrim die on the way to Rome, where he hopes to receive the benefits that the Pope has a right to bestow, the Pope is entitled to allow that pilgrim to receive the benefits as fully as if the pilgrimage had been completed, assuming, of course, that the man is worthy of their reception.

We shall have occasion later on to discuss the worship of saints. For the present it is enough to point out that no Pope ever can or will declare any one to be a saint, unless God Himself shows him to be so by conferring upon him extraordinary graces. No Pope, for instance, could canonize Henry VIII, nor has any Pope ever declared him to be damned. If you choose to consider Henry VIII a saint, well and good, but what guarantee have you that your opinion is correct? If we honour Francis of Assisi, or Benedict, or any one else as a saint, we wish to have assurance that we are not venerating some unworthy person, and we derive this assurance from the Holy Father's words. We know that he never declares any one to be a saint except after a most searching investigation and the removal of every possible doubt.

A Catholic looks upon the Pope as a loving Father who desires only to guide the souls intrusted to his charge along the way of salvation, who sympathizes with all in error, who longs for all to attain to the knowledge of the one truth, who prays and urges us to pray for all men, for those in authority, for pagans, Jews, and heretics, and who is the safeguard of truth and justice, mercy and love. Thus does every Catholic regard one whom a Protestant fancies to be a monster destroying the souls and bodies of men. If the Protestant were right, surely no one would be a Catholic. If the Pope resembled the false descriptions often given of him, no one would blame us should we abandon him; we need fear no persecution, but, on the contrary, many would applaud our action. As it is, however, we cling to the Pope with unfeigned affection, and this would be impossible if he were really what Protestants believe him to be. They assert that he lives in greater splendour than the mightiest monarchs, that his power is to theirs what the light of the sun is to that of the moon. "Secular rulers ought to know that they cannot hold office unless they are subservient to the Pope," etc., etc. We have already seen that formerly Catholic nations voluntarily ascribed to the Pope many rights that modern states do not accord to him, and the Popes have accepted these limitations to their power. It is both foolish and misleading to apply to the age in which we live, words uttered by some Pope under quite different circumstances.

Spiritual and Temporal Authority

The Popes and the Catholic Church have always taught that both the spiritual and temporal powers exist in accordance with God's will, and that each in its own sphere derives its authority from Him who said, "All power is given me in heaven and on earth." We do not maintain that the Pope's spiritual authority is superior to the state's temporal power, but we do believe that the kingdom of which Christ acknowledged Himself King, and which He appointed the Pope to govern as His representative, is superior to a state governed by such a man as Pilate; yet there is no natural antagonism between these two kingdoms, and it is God's will that they should coöperate in guiding men to their true goal in this life and the next. Every Christian sovereign is bound to fulfil the law of Christ and to govern his people in the spirit of Christ. In the Middle Ages kings and emperors often treated the Church as their servant rather than as their mother, and then the Popes enforced their rights vigorously, thus showing themselves to be benefactors of the people. Johann von Müller, a famous historian writes: "Gregory, Alexander, and Innocent raised a barrier against the tide that threatened to overflow the whole world. Their fatherly care raised up the hierarchy and insured the liberty of the various states."

Some years ago Woodrow Wilson, now President of the United States, delivered an address before the student body of Princeton University, lucidly setting forth the enormous service rendered by the Church to civil government during the Middle Ages. He said in part: "No society is renewed from the top; every society is renewed from the bottom. I can give you an illustration, concerning that that has always interested me profoundly. The only reason why government did not suffer dry rot in the Middle Ages under the aristocratic systems which governed them, was that the men who were the efficient instruments of government — most of the officials of government — the men who were efficient — were drawn from the Church, from that great Church body which we now distinguish from other church bodies as the Roman Catholic Church.

"The Roman Catholic Church then, as now, was a great democracy. There was no peasant so humble that he might not become a priest and no priest so obscure that he might not become the Pope of Christendom.

"Every chancellery in Europe, every court in Europe, was ruled by these learned, trained, and accomplished men, the priesthood of that great and then dominant Church.

"So, what kept government alive in the Middle Ages was this constant rise of sap from the bottom, from the ranks, from the rank and file of the great body of the people through the open channels of the Roman Catholic priesthood."

No Pope has ever pretended that he could distribute the kingdoms as he pleased; if he claimed the right to do so, he might simply have taken possession of them. We never heard that a Pope appointed a sovereign against the will of a nation. It would be well if Protestants studied the passages in Leo XIII's encyclicals, in which he lays down clearly the true relation between Church and state. (See especially the encyclical dated January 10, 1890, on the Duties of Christians as Citizens.)

Instead of referring to such contemporary utterances, however, Protestants prefer to quote sentences torn from their context, breathing the spirit of ages long past.

It is an absolute falsehood and calumny to assert that no oath sworn to heretics and heretical sovereigns and no compact or treaty made with them is binding in the eyes of the Popes.

There is another terrible charge frequently brought against the papacy, viz., that whoever refused allegiance to it was at its mercy and had to expect to undergo tortures worse than death. The constant references to the trials of the Waldensians and of heretics in Spain, France, England, etc., aim at increasing misinformation about Catholicism and at arousing bitter hatred against it.

Again, we are told that the Pope claims over all baptized persons the rights of ownership. These rights, however, simply consist in the fact that all validly baptized infants have received *Catholic* baptism, for there is no other. Luther happily kept the old Catholic form of baptism so that the infant who receives it, receives also the sanctifying grace which Christ connected with the sacrament, and the child is really received into the new life in which God is his father and the ancient Catholic and Apostolic Church his mother. Thus in a certain sense it is true that he belongs to the Pope and the Catholic Church, whether aware of it or not, until he voluntarily adopts some other faith. Even then he may continue in inculpable error and live according to his conscience, so that inwardly, though not outwardly, he is a member of the one Church of Christ. But, it may be asked, how does this unconscious membership of the Church reveal itself in the life of a baptized child or of a person in inculpable error? Surely it is in the fact that the way of salvation is open to them, and the Pope is far from wishing to persecute and condemn such persons; on the contrary the Church teaches that all those who have been baptized are her children, and she does this in order not to be forced to condemn them but rather to proclaim that even those can be saved who are not outwardly in communion with her.

Persecutions of Heretics

What can we say, however, of the terrible persecutions in which the Popes are alleged to have shed the blood of countless heretics? If there were to-day no power on earth capable of resisting them, would they not again proceed to torture and put to the rack all good Protestants?

The Church has certainly always tried to destroy error and must continue to do so, for Holy Scripture teaches that heresy, unbelief, and falling away from the faith are invariably grievous sins. "If any one preach to you a gospel besides that which you have received, let him be anathema" (Gal. i, 9). "If any man come to you, and bring not this doctrine, receive him not into the house, nor say to him 'God speed you'; for he that saith unto him 'God speed you' communicateth with his wicked works" (2 John, 10, 11). These are the words of Apostles, and St. Paul in another passage threatens the Corinthians that he may have to deal with them more severely, "according to the power which the Lord hath given me unto edification and not unto destruction" (2 Cor. xiii, 10).

The Church is bound to preserve the faith intrusted to her; she exists in order to defend it, and she can never sanction the teaching of a doctrine at variance with that which she has received. When St. Paul heard that Hymeneus and Alexander had made shipwreck concerning the faith, he did not say, "Let them believe whatever they like," but he "delivered them up to Satan, that they might learn not to blaspheme" (1 Tim. i, 30). Those who refuse to believe the words of Christ "shall drink of the wine of the wrath of God, . . . and shall be tormented with fire and brimstone . . . and the smoke of their torments shall ascend up for ever and ever, neither have they rest day nor night."

This terrible threat was not uttered by a Pope, but may be found in the Bible which Protestants profess to believe, and it is addressed to all who by their own fault abandon the true faith which can be but one. Is it not, therefore, a matter of the utmost importance to ascertain whether you possess this one true faith? And does it not behoove the Church, as guardian of this faith, to do her utmost to protect it and the faithful committed to her charge and to drive off the wolf when he approaches the sheepfold? Like St. Paul, the Church possesses this power for edification and not for destruction.

The Church is bound, therefore, to resist false doctrine, but the extirpation of the erring is not the best means of attaining this end. Unhappily this means was in past ages sanctioned and employed, but three remarks may be made on this subject: —

1. The bloody persecutions of heretics did not originate with the Catholic Church. In Roman law, with which the Popes had nothing to do, heresy was a serious offence against the state, "as it is far worse to offend God's majesty than the temporal power" (l. 63, cod. Theo., 16, 5). Forfeiture of possessions, exile, and even death were the penalties imposed by the civil courts for this offence. The first person condemned to death was Priscillianus in 385, but St. Martin implored the emperor not to allow the sentence to be carried out, and Pope Siricius also disapproved of it.

After the Roman empire with its legal system had passed away, the Popes undertook the task of reforming the administration of justice, and performed it in a way that has called forth the admiration of many non-Catholic scholars. Hinschius, a famous Protestant scholar, acknowledges the absolute justice of the proceedings of the Inquisition, although to uneducated persons the very name suggests an iniquitous means of obtaining a conviction at any cost.

Frederick Barbarossa and Frederick II put heretics to death, but Pope Innocent III, while allowing the emperors to persecute them, forbade torture. The Spanish Inquisition, of which we hear so much, was used by the sovereigns as a means of destroying persons they disliked, and the Popes did all in their power to check any injustice perpetrated by this court (cf. Hefele, *Cardinal Ximenes*).

As long as the Waldensians did not rise in rebellion, Pope

Innocent III allowed them to hold meetings in Metz and to read the Bible. Before the Battle of Cappel, Clement VII interceded for the Zwinglians, Pius V warned Philip II of Spain against shedding blood in the Netherlands, and the so-called dragonnades, a form of persecution inflicted upon Protestants in France, were condemned by Paul III, Francis I, and Innocent XI.

2. Although the Catholic Church and the Popes in their official capacity never had recourse to violent persecution of non-Catholics and never taught that sanguinary measures were permissible, we shall see that from the point of view of the rulers in the days when these persecutions took place, the means employed were in many cases quite justifiable. Among the Catholic nations of the Middle Ages, it was regarded as a most serious offence against the civil government for a man to fall away from the unity of faith, and consequently this offence, like many others, was punishable by death. This opinion was held even by the Hohenstaufens and other sovereigns notorious for their conflicts with the papacy. In many cases the false teachers were bitterly opposed to the civil order and incurred punishment on this account. Döllinger, for instance, says that the Cathari and Albigenses attacked marriage, family life, and the rights of property, and if they had triumphed the people would have lapsed into barbarism and pagan immorality. Was it not, therefore, incumbent upon all well-disposed persons to offer resistance and, if necessary, to have recourse to extreme measures in order to protect themselves against such a disaster?

3. An impartial study of history shows that whenever non-Catholics wielded the temporal power, they on their part treated Catholics with unparalleled severity and displayed intense fanaticism against them. We hear much of the sufferings of the Waldensians; why are the Cathari and Albigenses mentioned less frequently? The Waldensians were persecuted after they had allied themselves with these sects whose repression was a matter of absolute necessity for the state, for they went about plundering, killing, and destroying

churches, and by their doctrines they undermined the foundations of both ecclesiastical and civil life. It is most unfair to blame Catholicism for the cruelty that unhappily was shown in the struggle against them, and it is particularly unjust to regard the Popes as responsible for it (cf. Schmidt, *Histoire des Cathares*, etc., 1849). It can be read in Protestant books that, as late as 1655, four thousand innocent Waldensians were butchered in Piedmont, whereas the truth is that they began to attack and kill their Catholic neighbours, and in the fighting that ensued a few hundred, and not four thousand, Waldensians were slain. In the *Church Times*, an Anglican newspaper (1890, no. 385, p. 355), the accounts of this battle given by Leger, a Waldensian minister, are denounced as infamous calumnies.

Persecutions of Catholics

We hear much of the persecution that Protestants had to undergo, but comparatively little of the sufferings of faithful Catholics at the hands of Protestants. Luther himself says that rulers, princes, and lords, who belong to the canker of the Roman Sodom, ought to be assailed with all sorts of weapons, until men can wash their hands in their blood (Wittenb. ed., 1, 51 and 9, 24 b). Zwingli used to say of all who did not agree with him, that the Gospel thirsted for their blood. Calvin desired the institution of an "inquisition for the extermination of the race of heretics"; and between 1542 and 1546 the town council in Geneva banished seventy-six and put to death fifty-eight persons on the ground of their faith, whilst between eight and nine hundred others were arrested and thrown into prison where new tortures were constantly devised for them. Even Melanchthon praised Calvin for having burnt Servetus (*ep. 187 inter Calvini*).

In England Henry VIII caused thirty thousand people to be put to death on 'account of the Catholic faith. Cobbett, a Protestant historian, says of Queen Elizabeth: "Talk of Catholic persecution and cruelty! Where are you to find persecution and cruelty like this inflicted by Catholic princes?"

Within the space of six weeks she caused fifty thousand Catholics to be persecuted merely for the sake of their religion, and during the last twenty years of her reign no less than one hundred and forty-two priests were hanged, drawn, and quartered in England, whilst sixty-two prominent Catholic laymen also suffered martyrdom.

The events in France that preceded the horrible massacre of St. Bartholomew's night (which was organized solely by Queen Catherine) were such as to justify the adoption of stringent measures against the Huguenots, and the Church by no means recommended or sanctioned such proceedings. In the town of Orthoz the Huguenots had mercilessly butchered three thousand harmless Catholics; at St. Sever they had hurled two hundred priests down a precipice; Baron des Adrets forced his own children to wash their hands in Catholic blood, and Briquemant, one of the leaders of the Huguenots, used to wear a necklace made of the ears of slaughtered priests.

It is well known that Catholics were fiercely persecuted in the Netherlands, and in the northern kingdoms of Europe most severe penalties were inflicted upon them.

What right then have Protestants to accuse any one else of cruel persecutions? Would it not be better to let the sins and blunders of the past be forgotten? No one is justified in exciting the rabble by representing the Popes as responsible for all the bloodshed in past centuries, and as desirous to resume their work of butchery. Does any reasonable person really believe such statements to be true? Those who make them do ill service to the cause of truth, justice, and charity. Thousands of good Protestants know that the Pope is not the monster of cruelty and falsehood that he is painted. As Catholics we feel pain and sorrow at the abuse hurled at our Church and her supreme head, but our loyalty and love remain unaffected, and neither lies nor calumnies, neither bloodshed nor violence will make us abandon her.

IV. THE FORGIVENESS OF SINS

Protestants assert that the doctrines taught by the Roman Catholic Church regarding the forgiveness of sins are erroneous, inasmuch as she maintains that the punishment due to sin is remitted, not solely on the ground of Christ's merits but also on that of the superabundant merits of the saints and in return for good works performed by the sinner. She teaches, moreover, that the Pope claims power to apportion the merits of Christ and the saints, and thus to remit the punishment due to sin in this world and to relieve the souls in purgatory.

The Catholic Reply. The Catholic Church teaches that every sin, even the smallest, can be forgiven only through the merits of the death of our Lord on the Cross. In baptism all stain of sin is removed in virtue of these merits, but sins committed after baptism are forgiven in the Sacrament of Penance, again solely in virtue of Christ's merits. We read in Holy Scripture, however, that a debt of temporal punishment remains to be paid even after our sins are forgiven (2 Kings xii, 13, etc.). The everlasting punishment is remitted through our Saviour's merits, but the sinner himself must suffer the temporal punishment. In consequence of the Communion of Saints the merits of one can be applied to another, and the Church does this when she grants an indulgence (Matth. xvi, 19).

The Pope cannot assign the merits of Christ's death to whomsoever he will, but only to such who with contrite hearts desire to participate in them; and to these, if their sins and the everlasting punishment due them have been remitted, the Pope can grant remission of the temporal punishment by way of indulgence.

Indulgences can be applied to the souls in purgatory only by way of intercession. "Our good works benefit those only who in this life have deserved to be thus benefited" (St. Augustine, *Enchiridion*, cap. 110).

Protestants who base their doctrine upon Holy Scripture believe that sins are forgiven solely through the merits of Christ, for Isaias says, "The chastisement of our peace was upon him" (liii, 5), and St. John writes, "The blood of Jesus Christ cleanseth us from all sin" (1 John i, 7).

The Catholic Reply. This is precisely what the Catholic Church teaches with regard to Christ's merits. Luther denied, however, that any sanctification and renewal of the inner man was connected with the forgiveness of sins.

The Protestant Doctrine regarding the merits of the saints is that all require forgiveness and are saved through the blood of the Lamb (Apoc. vii, 14). Now people who need to have their own debts paid by another, are not able to pay those of others. Hence our Lord said to His disciples: "You also, when you shall have done all those things that are commanded you, say: 'We are unprofitable servants; we have done that which we ought to do'" (Luke xvii, 10).

The Catholic Reply is that of course all the saints owe their salvation to the Blood of Christ, and no one can make satisfaction for the sins of another; no Catholic questions these facts. But St. Paul wrote: "I rejoice in my sufferings for you, and fill up those things that are wanting of the sufferings of Christ, in my flesh for His body, which is the Church" (Col. i, 24). Hence it is possible for one Christian to suffer. instead of another, and if his own debts are paid out of an unmerited treasure of grace, he may pass on to his poorer brethren some of the abundance that he has received. All his merit is derived from Christ's merit, just as all the properties of the grape are derived from its growth on the vine.

Protestants maintain that according to Catholic doctrine purgatory is the place where those who die in faith and charity without, however, having attained to perfection, are detained, in order to be cleansed by suffering from every sin and to make satisfaction to God's justice for every fault for which they have not atoned in this life. This doctrine, like that of the superabundant merits of the saints, is the basis upon which the theory of indulgences rests, and is used as a means of gaining power and of extorting money from the deluded creatures who believe it.

The Catholic Reply. Our belief in the existence of a place of purgation is based upon reason, upon Holy Scripture, and the oldest Christian traditions (2 Mach. xii, 40–46). Our Lord, too, speaks of sins that shall not be forgiven either in this world or *in the world to come* (Matth. xii, 32). There must therefore be sins which can still be forgiven after death. That the doctrine regarding purgatory is used as a means of gaining money and influence is a malicious and spiteful misrepresentation of fact.

Protestants declare that there is nothing about purgatory in Holy Scripture, and that this doctrine is opposed to clear statements in the Bible such as Apoc. xiv, 13.

The Catholic Reply. Yet Martin Luther said in his Leipzig disputation that he was certain of the existence of purga-tory, and that it behooved men to help the poor souls detained there (Wittenberg ed., part 7, f. 7, and 132). We read in the Bible that it is a holy and wholesome thought to pray for the dead, that they may be loosed from sins (2 Mach. xii, 46). The fourteenth chapter of the Apocalypse contains a descrip- tion of the Church and those who persecute her at the end of the world, not at the close of the individual life. On the day of judgment all who have died in the Lord will undoubtedly rest from their labours. The Catholic doctrine is not at all incompatible with Apoc. xiv.

COMMENTARY

The Council of Trent excluded from the Catholic Church any who should maintain that man could be justified by his own works . . . independently of the grace of Jesus Christ (sess. 6, can. 1).

We must, therefore, seek elsewhere the difference between the Catholic and the Protestant teaching on the subject of forgiveness of sins.

The Catholic Church teaches, in accordance with Holy Scripture, that the justification of a sinner can be effected only through the merits of Christ. But she teaches further that by God's grace the sinner really becomes just, being inwardly renewed and sanctified, as St. Paul writes to the Corinthians (1 Cor. vi, 11), "You are washed, you are sanctified, you are justified in the name of our Lord Jesus Christ," and to the Romans (viii, 1), "There is therefore now no condemnation to them that are in Christ Jesus" (cf. also Tit. iii, 5). The Church tells us that in each baptized Christian a new life begins in which, by coöperation with grace, he can lay up a treasure in heaven (Matth. xix, 21). Nothing displeasing to God remains after baptism, for concupiscence is not sin but a consequence of sin; sometimes indeed it is called sin, but it is so only in the sense that it is a result of and incentive to sin. Whoever retains his baptismal innocence needs no indulgences and has no purgatory to undergo.

Indulgences affect the temporal punishment imposed by God after the sins committed by a baptized person have been forgiven (2 Kings xii, 13, 14). The Catholic Church declares that Christ bestowed upon her the power (Matth. xvi, 19) to release men from these penalties, but when she uses this power she again does nothing but to apply the merits of Christ to penitent sinners whose offences have already been pardoned by God, as St. Paul writes, "What I have pardoned . . . for your sakes have I done it in the person of Christ" (2 Cor. ii, 10).

When Catholics speak of the superabundant merits of the saints, in virtue whereof we can obtain remission of punishment due to our sins, they have no intention of setting these merits at all on a level with our Lord's, for those of the saints are only real and efficacious inasmuch as Christ Himself lived and worked in them (cf. Col. i, 24). When rightly understood, this teaching of the Church, which after all is not a dogma of faith, is far from underrating our Lord's merits and is based upon the living union between the Church and Christ who is her Head.

Luther and his followers departed from the doctrine taught in all the previous centuries, and maintained that baptism and regeneration do not really remove the natural sinfulness of man, who continues to be a sinner steeped in wickedness and damnable in God's sight. The righteousness of Christ is merely imputed to him, he is declared just, without in reality being so, and his sins are covered up, not removed. This doctrine is manifestly opposed to Holy Scripture (Rom. viii, 1). We may say that Protestantism promises to every one the most perfect plenary indulgence, since it is only necessary for a sinner to believe that merits not his own are imputed to him, so that they cover up his sins and unconditionally deliver him from all the consequences of sin in time and in eternity. There is no idea of the duty or possibility of his rendering himself worthy to receive such a boon.

Sin

Protestants maintain that they take a much more serious view than Catholics do of the corruption of the human heart, since they do not believe its natural sinfulness to be removed ' by baptism, and think that the warfare between the flesh and the spirit goes on incessantly, whilst even the regenerate crucify their lusts and concupiscences (Gal. v, 16-24). According to Catholic teaching, the Apostles term lust "sin" merely because it is the outcome of sin and disposes men to sin, whereas Protestants do not presume to declare anything not to be sin to which the Bible gives this name.

Thus Protestants claim to take a more serious view than we do of the corruption of the human heart! We need not discuss this point, but let us rather consider whether the Protestant doctrines regarding sin and redemption are more true, more in harmony with the word of God, and more sure to lead men to their eternal goal than are the doctrines of the Catholic Church. We shall soon discover that this is not the case.

The first fundamental mistake made by Protestantism is to ignore completely the moral nature of man. If the Protestant teaching were well established, it would deprive man of every reasonable disposition to recognize God as his own final end, and of all free will either to resist or coöperate with God's grace. Thus Luther says: "All that we do, is done not of our own free will, but of necessity" (*de serv. arb. Opp. lat.,* iii, f. 177); "We must do everything as God wills us to do

it, and our free will does nothing, since it is non-existent"
(Witt. ed., 6, p. 460). Melanchthon enlarges upon this theory
and writes: "God does everything, good and bad; He was the
author of the treachery of Judas as well as of the conversion
of Paul" (*Ep. ad Rom.*, cap. 8., 1522 ed.). The Reformers
held that man's whole nature was sin and nothing else. The
justice of Christ was imputed to him only outwardly, but on
this account man was no longer held guilty of sin. This doctrine may have originated in a profound sense of human
sinfulness but it is one-sided and exaggerated. It denies the
capability of man to improve and to become really just and
the friend of God, although this is indeed possible only through
Christ's merits. It is likely to encourage him to sin and to
abandon all efforts to lead a moral life; in fact Luther himself used to say, "Sin stoutly, but believe yet more stoutly."
Some Protestants have seen that this theory of the persistence
of natural sinfulness even in the just is a gross exaggeration,
and this has led them to deny that human nature is corrupt
at all and to reject the doctrine of original sin.

The Catholic Church falls into neither extreme. She takes
a most serious view of all sin, — of the sins committed by the
angels and by Adam as well as of the personal sins of men;
nor does she overlook the terrible consequences of sin, including those of original sin. She certainly does not view sin
lightly nor our struggles against it. No one can listen to the
instructions given at missions and retreats without being
aware of this fact. Nor does the Church make forgiveness
so simple and easy a matter as it would be if she merely said,
"Believe that Christ's merits are imputed to you, and then
all the evil results of your sin will be removed and you will
no longer be held guilty of it." No, she requires of us serious
and voluntary coöperation with God's grace, real conversion,
abandonment of sin, and the conquest of our inclination to
sin. She perceives the full malice and force of sin, but she
does not fail to see the magnitude and power of God's grace.
"Where sin abounded, grace did more abound" (Rom. v,
20). She does not think lightly of sin, but she recognizes the

omnipotence of divine grace. She believes that when Christ said to a leper, "Be thou cleansed," the man was really cured of his disease; and, in the same way, that when He says to a sinner, "Thy sins are forgiven thee," the sins are as completely removed as the leprosy was in the former instance. St. John baptized with water, Christ baptizes with fire and the Holy Spirit, and this baptism is the beginning of a new life, the resurrection from spiritual death. Nothing worthy of condemnation is left in those who are in Christ Jesus, for the Spirit bestows life in Him and delivers them from the law of sin and death (Rom. viii, 1, 2). The Church regards one who is justified as really risen with Christ and, being thus united with Christ, as able to perform good works acceptable in God's sight.

Having been taught by her divine Founder the true nature of sin, the Church does not presume to give this name to concupiscence which continues to exist even in baptized persons and is not really sin. It is true that St. Paul calls it sin in Rom. vii, but here, as in many other passages of Holy Scripture, it behooves us not to take the words too literally but to study St. Paul's teaching as a whole. In this chapter the Apostle depicts the unhappy state of an unbaptized person who is still contaminated with original sin, and in the next he extols the grace of Christ that can awaken such a person to a new life in which nothing is left worthy of condemnation, since sin is slain and the man becomes a child of God and an heir to heaven. In none of St. Paul's epistles is there any suggestion of a natural sinfulness remaining as actual sin in those who are justified, and although he speaks of concupiscence as sin, Catholics have never felt any doubt as to his meaning. St. James (i, 15) states the relation between concupiscence and sin quite plainly where he says, "When concupiscence hath conceived, it bringeth forth sin." Midway between evil desires and sin stands man's free will; he can yield to or resist the temptation; if he yields, sin results, but God summons every one to resist. St. Augustine points out that St. James distinguishes concupiscence and sin as being mother and daughter (*adv. Jul.*, l. 6, c. 15, n. 47) and remarks that concupiscence is called sin because it is a sin *to yield to it* (*de perf. just.*, n. 44). In the same way St. Paul says of one who receives the Lord's Body unworthily that he "eateth and drinketh judgment to himself." He does not mean that Holy Communion is actually judgment or condemnation, but he speaks of it thus, because it brings condemnation upon an unworthy communicant. So he calls concupiscence sin, because whoever *does not resist it*, sins. The Council of Trent declared with perfect truth (sess. 5, cap. 5) that the Catholic Church had never understood this passage to mean that concupiscence was actually a sin in the regenerate, but only that concupiscence was called sin because it was the outcome of sin and disposed a man to commit actual sin.

The Council of Trent recognized most fully that the warfare between the flesh and the spirit is unending, — no Catholic would deny it; but warfare is not sin; it involves the possibility of defeat, but also the possibility and hope of victory. He who succumbs to the dominion of sin, ceases to fight.

What would Luther say to the assertion that the regenerate crucify their lusts and concupiscences? He wrote: "Why should we torment ourselves with the attempt to make people good? Why should we trouble to keep the ten commandments, as they are unprofitable for salvation?" (*Table Talk*, *Aurif.*, f. 178) and again: "Only fools struggle to resist concupiscence with prayer, fasting, and other mortifications, for it is easy enough to get rid of temptations" (viz., by yielding to them). Luther's own words are significant, "provided women and girls are to be had" (*Works*, Jena, II, 216 b). The Catholic Church is in earnest when she insists upon crucifying the flesh; this doctrine has gained her much opposition, and many, thinking it too hard, have forsaken her in consequence. Yet the saints in the Catholic Church have always been conspicuous for their heroism in crucifying their lusts.

The Catholic View of Sin

Another assertion made by Protestants is that the Roman Catholic Church, and the Jesuit moral in particular, tends to minimize offences which even a Turk or a pagan would regard as sins. They say that the Pope sanctions the publication of books in which we read that excuses can be made for murder, adultery, immorality, fraud, and perjury.

We should be inclined to take the opposite view and to say that in the eyes of Protestants calumny is no sin provided it is directed against Catholics and especially against the Jesuits. "There is something repellent," said a non-Catholic in the *News-Advertiser*, Vancouver, B. C., "in the way in which some ministers discuss the Roman Catholic Church. . . The rancor exhibited by certain clerics toward what they are pleased to term 'Rome and all her works,' would be amusing if it were not so thoroughly malicious. I do not believe the Jews to be more bitterly persecuted than the Church of Rome. Persons go out of their way to abuse the Pope, and the charming reverence given to Christ's Mother and to the saints. It is a Church with many beautiful teachings, and I do not find its ministers railing at other religious institutions. Why, if religion be Christian, should some minister . . . mount to his pulpit to abuse his brother? It is illogical. And it wakes in every free, just mind a desire to see fair play — to speak the free word, to view with wide eyes the great sad, heaving world which contains so much suffering and so much love, and in which forever the generous and weary figure of the Christ hangs suspended 'twixt earth and heaven."

It is an outrageous calumny to say that either the Catholic Church as a whole or any influential party in the Church teaches that such sins are permissible or even excusable.

Protestants need only refer to any Catholic Catechism and to any explanation of the same, or to *The Perfect Christian* by St. Alphonsus, who is so often falsely represented as palliating vice, to see how Catholic children and Catholics in general are taught to feel hatred and abhorrence of all, even trifling, sins. It is impossible to find a single Catholic book of instruction or a single Catholic priest or catechist in the whole world who would venture to say that, under any circumstances whatever, murder, adultery, and perjury were only venial sins or not sins at all. The Jesuits, in harmony with the whole Church, teach that hatred, enmity, envy, uncharitableness, and voluntary indulgence in impure thoughts and desires are undoubtedly sinful, and that whosoever looks on a woman to lust after her, hath already committed adultery with her in his heart (Matth. v, 28), as our Lord taught. How then is it possible that the same persons should palliate or permit actions resulting from these evil thoughts?

What are we to say regarding the alleged books, sanctioned by the Pope and the ecclesiastical authorities, said to contain such abominable doctrines, inducing Catholics to regard as excusable some offences which even Turks and pagans know to be sins?

It is unhappily true that such books exist, and they poison the minds of thousands who cease to consider as sin that which is really sinful and leads to destruction. But these books are not used in the instruction of Catholic children, nor are they employed by Catholic confessors as a guide in the proper discharge of their judicial functions, nor, forsooth, are they published with the sanction of the Pope and the ecclesiastical authorities. The Catholic Church is often criticized for her hostility towards this kind of infidel literature, but the books to which Protestants refer are those written on the Catholic moral code for the instruction of confessors.

With regard to these books, inasmuch as they really contain Catholic doctrine, we may say they are in accordance with the principles of evangelical morality, and are written, not in order to lead the innocent astray, but in order to aid confessors in saving souls and in guarding them from sin. The writers have no intention of palliating any sin whatever, but of showing confessors how to judge of the magnitude of sins according to the principles of reason and the divine law.

To a confessor, books of this kind are as useful and necessary as textbooks of medicine are to a physician or books on law to a judge. One of these books, written by Father Gury, a Jesuit, has been described by Protestants as full of revolting doctrines, an abyss of filth and coarseness; but Georg Evers, a convert, formerly a Protestant minister, says of this work: "For the sake of gaining information, I read the chapter on the Sixth Commandment in Gury's book. What I found stated (in Latin), for priests dealing with difficult cases, stands in the same relation to Luther's disgusting obscenities as the advice given by a good, moral physician to the impure conversation of wantons."

It is a most complete distortion of the true facts to say that the Church of Rome under Jesuit influence teaches sin to be excusable, whereas Protestantism views it much more seriously. On the contrary, the Catholic Church, including the Jesuits, recognizes the full malice of sin as being a voluntary and infinite wrong committed against God. The Catholic Church makes light of no sin, and she teaches that the only sure way of overcoming it is to be pure and honest even in small matters; she cherishes virtue such as the world does not know, and she leads the elect on to the highest point of sanctity.

The Forgiveness of Sin

Protestants acknowledge that the so-called Tridentine decree contains much that is true regarding the forgiveness of sins, but they ascribe this fact to the presence at the Council of many honest men who, they imagine, were really evangelicals at heart. They maintain that the decisions on this article of faith were expressed in ambiguous language owing to the presence of some who held other opinions. Nevertheless the Council of Trent teaches that sins are only partially removed by the merits of Christ, and partially by those of the saints and by the satisfaction made by the sinner himself; such a doctrine being, according to the Protestant view, opposed to Holy Scripture (Ps. xlix (xlviii), 8, 9; Ephes. ii, 8, 9).

What extraordinary ideas on the subject of Catholicism possess the minds of those who are not of our faith! The

Council of Trent was convoked chiefly in order to put an end to various abuses in the Church, and to defend the ancient truths of Catholicism against modern assailants, most of whom were followers of Luther. Yet these Protestants imagine that many persons present at the Council were really evangelical at heart. If by evangelical they mean believers in the Gospel of Christ, then not only many but all of the learned men assembled at Trent were genuinely evangelical, as are the Pope and all good Catholics, including the Jesuits, at the present day. But not a single one of them was a Protestant; they all unanimously held the old Catholic faith based on Scripture and tradition. If one point in this faith finds favour with a Protestant, who fails to discover in it any of the horrible misrepresentations which he has from childhood associated with Catholicism, he at once assumes that it is not Catholic doctrine at all but a fragment of Protestantism. It would be more correct to take a contrary view. Protestants often retain more of the Catholic truth than they themselves are aware of, and on many points hold thoroughly Catholic opinions. All that is good, noble, pure, and holy in the teaching of the Reformers, was carried with them when they forsook the Catholic Church, their early home.

There is no ambiguity in the decisions of the Council of Trent; they contain the true doctrine, stated clearly in all its aspects and bearings. They plainly ascribe all the merit in the forgiveness of sins to Jesus Christ, our Mediator and Redeemer, but they do not deny that a sinner possesses free will whereby he can coöperate in the work of his salvation.

There is an inexplicable confusion in the minds of Protestants between the guilt of sin and the punishment due to it. The Council of Trent declared it to be the Catholic belief that no human merit suffices to release a sinner from even a slight sin. Great care was taken not to suggest in any way a failure to appreciate the importance of Christ's satisfaction or to diminish and limit its efficacy. Yet no sinner can share in this satisfaction unless he himself coöperate with it. There is clear evidence in Holy Scripture that the temporal punishment due to sin may remain after the sin itself is forgiven (e.g., 2 Kings xii, 13). The Church formerly imposed very severe penances upon sinners and, like St. John the Baptist, required them to bring forth fruit worthy of penance, yet this satisfaction derived all its value from Christ, since we are unable to do anything of ourselves, although we can do all things in Christ who strengtheneth us (2 Cor. iii, 5; Phil. iv. 13). In Christ we live, and in Him we merit, and if we suffer with Him, we shall be also glorified with Him (Rom. viii, 17). How can Protestants boast that the regenerate amongst them crucify their lusts and passions, and at the same time reproach the Catholic Church for ascribing some value and importance to our suffering in union with the atonement made by Jesus Christ?

It is a misrepresentation to assert that Catholics believe the merits of Christ to suffice only partially for the removal of sins, so that the merits of the saints and the satisfaction made by the sinner himself are required in addition. The Council of Trent declared that all our glory is in Christ, in whom we bring forth fruit worthy of penance, which derives all its efficacy from Him, and through Him is offered to and accepted by our heavenly Father. The merits of the saints are not mentioned at all in connection with personal penance, and we are far from supposing that they are needed to augment those of Christ. We read, however, in Holy Scripture that God would have spared Sodom at Abraham's intercession, had there been ten just men in the city.

Finally, when Protestants say that Catholic doctrine is manifestly contrary to Holy Scripture, and refer to two passages in support of their assertion, we may reply that in Ephes. ii, 8, 9 St. Paul's meaning is: Jesus alone is our Redeemer, His grace alone saved us without our previously meriting anything. No Catholic denies this, but the words contain no reference at all to the value of penitential works performed by a sinner who falls into sin after baptism and by God's grace repents and is converted. The Protestant translation of Ps. xlix (xlviii), 8 is, "None of them can by any means redeem his brother." The reference is to redemption from sin, but the context of the Psalm shows that the author was speaking of death.

Indulgences

Protestants believe that the Popes claim to have received power from Christ to remit the temporal punishment required by divine justice, by drawing on the treasury of the Church, i.e., on the superabundant merits of Christ and the saints. They can also by the same means afford alleviation and release to the souls in purgatory through the mediation of the living. A papal indulgence is, according to Protestants, the remission of so many days' or years' detention in purgatory; sometimes part of the *guilt* is remitted, but at other times the Pope forgives all sins indiscriminately. Sometimes the living enjoy the benefits of an indulgence, but more frequently they obtain these benefits for the dead, and the latter kind of indulgence is the most important and most highly prized.

It is true that the Popes, acting as the vicars of Christ, claim to have authority to remit the temporal punishment due to sin, but their claim is based upon our Lord's words to St. Peter: "Whatsoever thou shalt loose on earth, it shall be loosed also in heaven" (Matth. xvi, 19). These words refer to all that can hinder the soul's entrance to heaven, and therefore include temporal punishment. The history of Moses and of David shows that such punishment is imposed by God even when the sin is forgiven. All the Fathers of the Church, as even Calvin admits, unanimously declare that a forgiven sinner still has to make satisfaction. In the ordinary course of things the sinner has to endure his punishment, but it may be remitted as a special favour. Every child knows this who, by displaying greater love and more perfect obedience, tries to please its parents and prevent them from inflicting punishment. Every criminal knows that the sovereign can use his right to pardon and commute, diminish or quash the sentence pronounced against him. Hence it is surely not surprising that the supreme head of the Church should claim a similar privilege. In the Sacraments of Baptism and Penance he has full authority to release a sinner from the eternal punishment due to sin; he acts in the name of Jesus Christ, and applies the merits of Christ to every sinner who does what is required of him; why then should not the Pope be able to remit less severe penalties? Protestants assume that they can avail themselves of all the merits of Christ, and that they are free from all guilt and punishment if they only believe the justice of Christ to be imputed to them. Thus they really grant the most complete plenary indulgence to themselves unconditionally, whereas a Catholic, although he relies equally upon the merits of Christ, expects them to be conferred upon him only in the manner prescribed by our Lord Himself.

Protestants are apt entirely to overlook the fact that indulgences are granted under quite definite conditions. They seem to fancy that the Pope bestows them just as he likes, although he is bound to act in this, as in other matters, only as Christ's representative and in accordance with His will. All Catholic theologians are agreed in thinking that it is not permissible to grant indulgences without sufficient reason, and they would be invalid should a Pope attempt to grant them thus. Indulgences of a thousand years are, as Benedict XIV declared, probably not genuine. Another point overlooked by Protestants is that any one anxious to gain an indulgence must faithfully comply with certain conditions, the first being invariably that he must be in the state of grace. If the punishment due to his sins is to be remitted, those sins must previously be removed by means of true contrition or, in the case of grievous sins, by means of the Sacrament of Penance. No indulgence renders superfluous contrition, penance, and true purpose of amendment; the fact that the punishment is diminished or remitted ought to stimulate the sinner to make fresh efforts to overcome his faults. The prescribed good works have to be faithfully performed, and the chief of these is prayer for the welfare of Holy Church. Finally, as Tetzel, the much calumniated preacher of indulgences, said, "the people ought constantly to be reminded that God saves us, not for the good works that we do, but in

His own most holy compassion" (Janssen, *An meine Kritiker*, 14), and that "no one deserves an indulgence, although he may be truly penitent and in charity with God, and whoever does good works for love of God, directs them towards God in his life."

It is an outrageous falsehood to say that the Pope sometimes remits part of the guilt of sin, and at other times remits the sins altogether. Let me repeat again most emphatically that the Pope, when he grants an indulgence, has no intention of forgiving any sin either partially or completely.

Purgatory

Protestants say that of all indulgences those applicable to the souls in purgatory are the most important and most highly prized. They declare that the Catholic doctrine regarding purgatory is an insult to Jesus Christ, who has made atonement for our sins, and that those who believe souls to be purified by the tortures of purgatory forget that amendment is not the necessary result of suffering.

Is it not a fact that many Protestants pray for the dead and that even in funeral orations they refer to faults not wholly eradicated during life? Is this not a proof of the persistence of the old Catholic feeling with regard to the departed? We trust that they are too good for hell, but perhaps they are not yet fit for heaven whither nothing unclean can gain admission. If they are still unable to enjoy the beatific vision, ought death to be a barrier to the charity that never faileth? St. Paul hoped to be delivered from captivity by the prayers of the faithful (Philemon 22), and prayed that the Lord would grant unto Onesimus "to find mercy in that day" (2 Tim. i, 18), and in the same way every Christian hopes by his prayers to help those dear to him even after their earthly life is over. At first Luther did not deny the existence of purgatory, and believed that the departed could benefit by the prayers of their survivors, but subsequently his other doctrines forced him to oppose the constant faith of the Church, based though it is on both the Old and the New Testament, and he finally taught that there was no purgatory. St. Augustine, referring to Matth. xii, 32, says, "there is forgiveness of sins also in the next life," and, "The prayer of the righteous is heard in aid of those Christians who have departed from this life, and are not so wicked as to be condemned, nor so good as to be able immediately to enter heaven" (*de civ. Dei*, l. 21, c. 24).

What can be said in answer to the statement that faith in purgatory is an insult to Jesus Christ? A sinner insults Christ by his evil works, and it is precisely on this account that he suffers the punishment which he deserves, that God may be glorified and receive the honour due to Him.

Jeremy Taylor, the famous Protestant Bishop, author of *Holy Living* and *Holy Dying*, and incidentally an inveterate opponent of many of our cherished doctrines, on the subject of prayers for the dead admitted a complete acceptance:

"It is very considerable, that since our blessed Saviour did reprove all the evil doctrines and traditions of the scribes and Pharisees, and did argue concerning the dead and the resurrection against the Sadducees, yet He spake no word against this public practice of intercession, but left it as He found it; which He who came to declare to us all the will of His Father would not have done if it had not been innocent, pious, and full of charity" (*Selections from Theology*, Section XX). Elsewhere he says: "The dead people, even to the day of judgment, are the subject of a misery, the object of God's mercy, and therefore fit to be commemorated in the duties of our piety and charity. . . . It being certain that they have a need of mercy, and it being uncertain how great their need is, it may concern the prudence of charity, to be the more earnest, as not knowing the greatness of their necessity" (*Ibid.*).

Again, we are charged with forgetting that amendment is not a necessary result of suffering. The flames of hell are not intended to effect amendment but to punish, and the pains of purgatory are also punitive. No amount of punishment improves one who is hardened in vice, yet we do not on that account close our prisons, and a loving child who thoughtlessly or recklessly has offended its parents may certainly be improved by punishment. The penance which a sinner, conscious of his guilt, accepts without hesitation, really purges and cleanses him. We see here the difference between hell and purgatory.

William Mallock writes: "As to this doctrine of Purgatory — which has so long been a stumbling block to the whole Protestant world — time goes on, and the view men take of it is changing. It is becoming fast recognized on all sides that *it is the only doctrine that can bring a belief in future rewards and punishments into anything like accordance with our notions of what is just and reasonable.* So far from its being a superfluous superstition, it is seen to be just what is demanded at once by reason and morality, and a belief in it to be not only an intellectual assent, but a partial harmonizing of the whole moral ideal" (*Is Life Worth Living?* Chap. XI).

Indulgences Applied to Souls in Purgatory

Protestants tell us that the sufferings of purgatory are described as excruciating, but nevertheless the Popes make it quite easy for people in this world to deliver their relatives and friends from this place of torment by means of innumerable indulgences.

The Popes have defined nothing with regard to the alleged excruciating sufferings of purgatory, and we do not know of what they consist; though the common sense of Christians certainly suggests that to a soul who loves God and aspires to Him as her highest good, it must be intense pain to be held back from Him by the consequences of her own folly and sin.

Power to grant indulgences was given to the papacy by its Founder, and the possibility of applying them by way of intercession to the souls in purgatory is in harmony with the universal belief of Christians in the Communion of Saints and in the value of intercessory prayer. The members of the primitive Church were firmly convinced that "the continual prayer of a just man availeth much" (James v, 16).

Whether or no the Popes have made it very easy to release

souls from purgatory is another question. It is not for us to decide whether God is really willing to accept our good works when they are the outcome of our faith and charity, nor do we know how far He does so in each individual case, nor whether He applies them to the souls in purgatory. Conditions must be fulfilled, both on our side and on that of the departed, if it is to be possible. The Catholic Church does not represent it as an easy matter to gain a plenary indulgence for oneself. It requires absolute freedom from even venial sin and from all attachment to sin, and in the same way the soul, to whom we intend to apply an indulgence, must be in a fit state to receive this benefit.

We are assured that when we pray with confidence our prayer is not in vain, and we know that in the third century St. Perpetua, being in prison, prayed for her dead brother, for she wrote, "I trusted that my prayers would alleviate his torments" (cf. Cap. 7 of her *Acts*, in which she relates how her brother appeared to her, thus confirming her belief that he had really been released through her intercession).

These alleged false doctrines of the Catholic Church are, according to Protestants, what induced Luther to come to the rescue of poor deluded people, sunk in superstition or vice, and to publish his ninety-five theses, in which he declares faith and repentance to be the way of forgiveness.

This is a mistake; it was not the Catholic doctrine regarding indulgences that aroused Luther's indignation, but the caricature of this doctrine as generally drawn by non-Catholics. Does not the seventy-first of Luther's theses contain the clear statement: "Let him who speaks against the truth of the papal indulgence be cursed and condemned"? Did not Luther himself assure Tetzel during his illness that the strife had not begun about him, but was "a child of quite different parentage"? (*de Wette*, I, 336.)

Nor was Luther incited to his rebellion by the abuses connected with preaching the indulgences. We Catholics are quite aware that there were abuses, and that misunderstandings of the nature of indulgences prevailed, and the Popes had recognized these facts and taken measures to check the evil. If Luther had really protested against abuses and misunderstandings, he would have a claim upon our gratitude. But the truth is that he only used these things as a welcome excuse for inveighing against the Holy See and its authority, and for openly proclaiming his own erroneous opinions on the subject of justification by faith alone. In order to represent Luther as coming to the rescue of poor misguided souls, Protestants assume that the Catholic doctrine regarding indulgences had plunged the people into superstition and vice, but such was by no means the case. Tetzel gave instructions to those who were preaching the indulgence, that they must impress upon the faithful the fact that every indulgence is granted primarily for the glory of God, and that no one can gain an indulgence who is not truly penitent and filled with love of God, and he went on to say: "The indulgence is gained by such as are in a state of true contrition and charity, which do not suffer them to remain idle and inactive, but spur them on to serve God." "It is certain that the indulgence is gained by Christian, God-fearing, and pious people and not by the indolent and reckless" (Janssen, *An meine Kritiker*, 14).

Cardinal Wiseman was in Rome on the occasion of a comparatively recent proclamation of an indulgence, and in writing to some friends he expressed the wish that they could have seen the crowds outside the confessionals and the innumerable communicants at the altars. Stolen property was, he said, returned, and hardened sinners were converted. He thought that his correspondents, had they witnessed all this, could have judged for themselves whether or no the proclamation of an indulgence really encouraged men to commit sins with impunity.

The Protestant Plenary Indulgence

It is, I repeat, absolutely false to say that the proclamation of an indulgence ever plunged unhappy souls into vice

100

or impiety, yet such a statement is frequently made for the purpose of keeping alive the prejudices against Catholicism. History proves that the people were misled and plunged into vice by a preaching of quite another kind, viz., by the sermons of Luther himself and his followers. He did indeed proclaim a plenary indulgence, when he taught that a man need only have faith in order to go straight to heaven, neither contrition nor good works being required of him. Such an indulgence as this could not, of course, be applied to the departed, as it rendered purgatory altogether unnecessary. Luther soon discovered the effect that this teaching had upon the people, and complained bitterly of it. "We live," he wrote towards the close of his life, "in Sodom and Babylon, and among all classes lawlessness, together with all kinds of vice, sins, and scandals, is now much greater than ever before." "Who would have begun to preach, if we had known beforehand that so much misery and wickedness would result from it?" (Janssen, op. cit., 33.) Böhmer, a Protestant writer, called the Reformation the source of all the evils from which we now suffer. Droysen, an antagonist of the Catholic Church, makes the following confession: "Through the ecclesiastical revolution there arose fearful disorders and confusion; the writings of the Reformers abound in pitiful lamentations over the growth of wickedness, usury, licentiousness, and every kind of sin" (op. cit.). No one could read carefully all the evidence on this subject that Janssen has collected, without arriving at an opinion different from that usually held by Protestants on the subject of the results of Catholic and Lutheran teaching respectively. Lutheranism requires a believer to feel absolute certainty of salvation; Catholicism teaches that no one in this world can possess complete assurance that he is saved, but that all ought to work out their salvation with fear and trembling, as St. Paul says: "I am not conscious to myself of anything, yet am I not hereby justified, but He that judgeth me is the Lord" (1 Cor. iv, 4).

The teaching of the Catholic Church on the subject of indulgences leads neither to despondency nor to carelessness, but it encourages a spirit of penance and so brings men to Christ. No Catholic ever expects to secure his salvation by means of indulgences. He may never have tried to gain one and yet be saved, for an indulgence is a benefit, a favour, the remission of the temporal punishment due to sin, but it is nothing more. A good Catholic no doubt values indulgences for what they are worth, but both in life and in death he relies solely upon God and his holy faith.

If there were no judicial authority in the Church, and if the utterances of her supreme ruler had no value in the sight of God, why should Christ have spoken of power to bind and to loose, and of feeding His sheep? We know well enough that papal bulls condemn no one, that God alone will be the judge of our souls, yet at the same time we trust that He had some good purpose in committing us, during our life on earth, to the charge of those to whom He said, "He that heareth you, heareth me, and he that despiseth you, despiseth me." Supposing our own conscience should urge us to adopt Luther's tenets, is it not possible that God might judge us otherwise than we should judge ourselves? Every Catholic knows who it is that has atoned for his sins and saved him from eternal damnation; he relies upon Christ alone, not on any indulgence, nor on the merits of any saint, nor upon any satisfaction that he himself can make. He knows, however, that he will not be taken to heaven as if he were an inanimate clod with no will of its own, and he recognizes purgatory as created by God, in His justice and love, in order that men may be saved. Purgatory was not invented by one of the Popes, but was designed by Him who cannot endure that anything unclean should enter heaven, and yet will not extinguish the smoking flax. Every Catholic believes that charity does not end at death. He is far from supposing that he is free to sin lustily, if only he has plenty of faith and gets plenty of indulgences or induces others to gain them for him. He knows to whom he is answerable, and he has been taught as a child to say, whenever he hears Holy Mass: "My Jesus, I will live for Thee; my Jesus, I will die for Thee; living and dying I am Thine."

V. FAITH AND GOOD WORKS

Protestants assert that, according to Roman Catholic doctrine, faith is nothing more than a belief in the revelations and promises of God.

The Catholic Reply. The Catholic Church teaches that there is such a thing as dead faith, which excludes hope and charity, and even the devils possess this faith (James ii, 19), but it does not suffice for salvation. Justifying faith must include heartfelt confidence in God and the charity whence contrition and purpose of amendment proceed.

The Protestant Doctrine is that faith is not merely a belief in God's revelations and promises, but is at the same time a heartfelt confidence that God in His mercy, for the sake of Christ's merits, will deign to have compassion upon us and make us just and blessed, as St. Paul says, "With the heart we believe unto justice" (Rom. x, 10). True faith worketh by charity (Gal. v, 6), and is fruitful in good works (James ii, 18).

The Catholic Reply. This is not Luther's doctrine, for he taught that salvation was by faith alone, i.e., by the confidence felt by the sinner that God had forgiven him. Luther insisted upon excluding charity and good works from faith. The statement given above is the Catholic definition of faith, the only difference being that the Catholic Church does not, like Luther, ascribe to faith power to justify and save.

Protestants maintain that the Roman Church teaches that by means of good works we can make satisfaction for our sins, thus ensuring their forgiveness and our salvation.

The Catholic Reply. Such a doctrine is altogether contrary to the Council of Trent, which condemned all who taught that man could be justified by his own works without divine grace (sess. 6, can. 1). The Catholic Church insists that man cannot be saved by faith alone, i.e., by dead faith, but she insists also that he cannot be saved by works alone, although good works are expedient, necessary, and meritorious. The necessity and meritorious character of good works is taught on almost every page of Holy Scripture, but especially in Matth. xxv and James ii.

Protestants believe that a man in the state of grace may perform really good works without being able to atone for his sins and deserve salvation, for St. Paul says: "By grace you are saved through faith, and that not of yourselves, for it is the gift of God, not of works, that no man may glory" (Ephes. ii, 8, 9).

The Catholic Reply. On the last day our Judge will admit to heaven those who have done good works, and exclude those who have neglected to do them (Matth. xxv). Hence the saints will owe their salvation to their own works conjointly with our Saviour's grace. St. Paul's words in Ephes. ii refer plainly to works performed by Christians before their conversion, hence these works could not be the outcome of faith.

Protestants assert that Catholics extol, as good works, almsgiving, fasting, saying the rosary, going on pilgrimages, visiting certain churches, the practice of various mortifications, taking religious vows, founding religious houses, and altogether observing the rules laid down by the Church.

The Catholic Reply. This is a most misleading statement of what we believe; it suggests that, in our opinion, all the merit of good works consists in the mechanical performance of outward actions, that the rules laid down by the Church take precedence of God's commandments, and that it is a matter of indifference for what reason the good works are performed, whether for love of God, or from a sense of our own sinfulness, or from force of habit, or even from motives of hypocrisy.

The real teaching of the Catholic Church is this: A work is rendered good in the sense of meritorious by the grace of God which prompts its performance; hence in order to be good in this sense, a work must be performed by one in the state of grace, it must be in accordance with God's will, and must be done with the intention of pleasing Him (Matth. vi, 1). The good works especially extolled by the Catholic Church, as well as in Holy Scripture, are prayer, fasting, and almsgiving (Tob. xii, 8; Matth. vi), obedience to the commandments of God, fulfilment of one's duties in life, and patience in suffering.

Protestants tell us that they describe as good works those which proceed from the conversion of the heart to God (such conversion being effected by the Holy Spirit), and also those which are performed in compliance with God's law as contained in the Bible.

The Catholic Reply. This again is Catholic doctrine. Luther, however, and his followers recognized no true conversion of the heart to God, effected by the Holy Spirit; they thought it impossible to fulfil the law of God, and regarded good works as useless, if not actually harmful.

COMMENTARY

Luther taught explicitly that justification is alone by faith that lays hold of Christ through the words of Holy Scripture, and not by the faith that includes charity (*Werke*, Wittenb., i, 47); those who wish to add love to faith are, in Luther's opinion, "ignorant and blundering asses." When Melanchthon quietly reminded him of St. Paul's words regarding the necessity of charity, Luther called him a Mameluke for agreeing with the papists in laying stress upon the coöperation of charity and hope (Plank, *Gesch. d. Entsteh.*, vi, 80). Luther would not tolerate any allusion to good works and goes so far as to say: "Faith that is connected with works does not justify; however trivial the works may be, it ceases to be faith" (*Epp. Aurif.*, tom. I, fol. 345 b). When some one remarked that faith ought to be living and active, he called this assertion "a wretched, patched-up phrase" (*Werke*, Walch, XVII, 840).

At the present time Protestants admit the truth of much which Luther most decidedly rejected, and we should view this action with joy, if only the very truths that the Catholic Church always has upheld and defended were not now brought forward as the triumphant results of the Reformation.

Luther did not trouble about a true conversion of the heart to God, effected by the Holy Spirit. He wrote that a Christian was not under the law but free, not only from the Pope's abominations and the blasphemous enactments of men, but also from all the control that God's law had over us (*Ep. ad Gal.*, Wittenb., *Werke*, I, 229): "Christ gave us no commandments" (f. 216), and "if you should imagine Christ to be a judge or legislator, ready to demand an account of the manner in which you have spent your life, you may be perfectly sure that it is not Christ, but the very devil himself" (216 b). The Pope was obliged to condemn Luther's theory that a just man sinned whenever he did a good work, and that a good work was at least a venial sin (Wittenb., VII, 117 b).

The Object of Faith

Protestants give the following as one of the chief differences between their doctrines and those of the Roman Catholic Church: Protestants regard faith as an acceptation of God's word revealed in Holy Scripture, whilst Roman Catholics, though they accept God's word as an object of faith, lay stress on the importance of believing everything taught by the Holy Roman Church.

This statement creates in the mind of the reader an impression that Catholicism sets human on a level with divine utterances, or even allows the former to take precedence of the latter. Yet the Vatican Council declared faith to be a supernatural virtue by means of which we accept, in reliance upon God's grace, whatever He has revealed, and we believe it, not because our reason recognizes it as the truth, but because God's word is eminently worthy of credence. The word of God, in the full meaning of the term, is for us Catholics the sole object of faith.

Because God's revelations were revealed and intrusted to men, and because Christ appointed His Church to be the infallible guardian and teacher of the faith, as is plain from

Holy Scripture, we believe what the Holy Roman Church calls upon us to believe. We believe in the word of God as it is recorded in the Bible and preserved in the tradition of the Church, but these are not two distinct objects of belief, nor is one the word of God and the other the word of man, but we accept the whole word of God from the Church to whom it was intrusted. This word cannot vary and be adapted to the opinions of men, and the Church cannot teach anything else but what God has spoken and revealed, nor can she ever contradict what stands written in Holy Scripture any more than an ambassador can alter the message that he is sent to deliver, or a judge give a sentence not in accordance with the law that it is his duty to interpret and enforce.

As God does not speak to each individual, we should have no means of attaining to a full and assured faith unless we possessed an infallible teacher of faith and an interpreter of the written word of God. Every bond of union between the faithful would soon be severed, and every reason for assured faith would vanish, if the Church ceased to insist upon unity and if our adherence to her doctrines were made optional. Hence St. Paul earnestly appeals to the Corinthians, in the name of our Lord Jesus Christ, "all to speak the same thing, that there be no schisms," and to be "in the same mind and in the same judgment" (1 Cor. i, 10).

This necessary unanimity in faith is possible then only when it is derived from the divine word preserved in the Church of Christ. Who has ever derived his faith from Holy Scripture alone? Not the Apostles or their contemporaries and disciples; nor did even Luther receive the Bible by itself, with the interpretation assigned to it for centuries in the Catholic Church. Indeed, he himself desired his followers not to believe the Bible alone, but to accept his views upon it. "I will not have my teaching criticized by any one," he wrote, "not even by angels. Whoever refuses to accept it, cannot be saved" (*Werke*, Erlangen, 28, 144). And again: "No human being ever taught like Luther." "I, Dr. Martin Luther," he said, "will have it so, I am wiser than the whole world" (Wittenb. ed., V, 107). When some one reproached him for inserting the word *alone* in his translation of Romans iii, 28, he said: "If a papist tries to make a fuss about this word, tell him outright that Martin Luther intends it to stand. A papist and an ass are one and the same thing" (*Deutsche Werke*, V, 171). In fact he declared frankly: "I care nothing for all the texts of Scripture [which speak of good works], Christ is on this [i.e., my] side" (Wittenb., ed. I, 146, 147). Luther required the preachers of his doctrines to conform exactly to his views (Plank, *Gesch. des prot. Lehrbegriffs*, II, 385, 387; IV, 67). Therefore his followers were not allowed to believe the Bible alone, but also Luther's opinions and interpretations. Luther asserted, though he could not prove, his own infallibility, in opposition to the real infallibility of the teaching authority in the Catholic Church based on Scripture and tradition, and in opposition also to Holy Scripture itself.

Most Protestants of the present day do not believe merely what they find in the Bible, but they accept the teaching of many men, for which the Bible contains no justification. They put faith in Luther, or in their own ministers, or in some modern line of thought, or in their own prejudices inherited from their forefathers. We Catholics, however, put faith only in the truth revealed by God, and in accepting this we hope to receive God's grace, to please Him, and to find salvation.

The Catholic Understanding of Faith

Protestants tell us that it is questionable whether, according to Catholic doctrine, earnest confidence in God's mercy forms part of the right faith. Faith may indeed be the first step towards justification, but it does not go far, since the Council of Trent affirmed it to be possible for a man to be a Christian and possess this faith without having any life, charity, or enjoyment of divine grace.

Holy Scripture contains several clear allusions to a dead faith, compatible with the state of God's wrath, for the devils possess faith of this kind. It is, however, worthless for salvation, being like a dead body without a soul. As soon as God's grace begins to affect the sinner, it behooves him voluntarily to coöperate with it, for it rests with him whether God's gift is really to be his salvation or to remain dead and unprofitable. His faith must be quickened to life, and fear, contrition, purpose of amendment, confidence in and, above all, love of God must be added to it. Faith, alive through charity, is the root and foundation of justification; and when it is brought into relation with justification and salvation, hearty confidence in God's grace and true love of God must inevitably be associated with it.

Luther's real views regarding justification by faith alone are obscure. On the one hand he denies that faith can remain dead, since he believes it to be exclusively God's work in man. A sinner cannot, in Luther's opinion, voluntarily accept the faith, but his will is like a horse that submits to the rider whether he be God or the devil. Hence faith once bestowed by God cannot remain dead. On the other hand Luther was most careful to eliminate from faith all activity manifesting itself in hope or charity; in faith, as he conceived of it, there was to be nothing human, nothing voluntary, nothing pleasing to God. "Faith alone justifies," was his dogma, "faith which apprehends Christ through the word, not the kind of faith which includes charity" (*Deutsche Werke*, Wittenberg, I, f. 47 b). Therefore, according to Luther, charity ought to be altogether excluded as having nothing to do with the work of justification.

This was indeed a new faith, unknown to previous generations, a kind of faith that was not the dead faith capable of remaining in the soul, though charity, grace, and supernatural life may all be lacking, nor yet a faith quickened by charity and manifesting itself actively in good works. What sort of faith then was this new faith of Luther's? It was undoubtedly a dead faith, such as St. James describes; Luther's art had no power to call it to life. There is no intermediate state between life and death, and Luther's faith was dead, incapable of leading to salvation. His own followers, happily oblivious of his real opinions, have to a great extent abandoned this doctrine upon which Luther himself insisted most emphatically, and have returned to the old Catholic view of faith. They are far from acknowledging this to be the case, for they persist in regarding the Catholic Church as the mother of all error and Catholic doctrines as falsehoods devised by men. Hence on this, as on other points, they misrepresent the Catholic Church, and attack, as being monstrous errors, doctrines that she has never taught, whilst they extol, as truths peculiar to Protestantism, things that they really owe to Catholic teaching.

Faith and Good Works

Protestants tell us that it is the special glory of their Church to teach that men are justified and saved solely through faith in Jesus Christ and not through any merit due to good works. They declare that Roman Catholicism attaches vast importance to good works, and teaches that by their means sin can be completely removed, and further graces and even eternal life can be merited.

The Catholic teaching on the subject of good works is perfectly clear, but Protestants do not state it intelligibly. What we understand by good works are all the actions and sufferings collectively of one who is a child of God, being regenerate through grace, or all the good fruits which Christ said every good tree must bring forth (Matth. vii, 17). We know that our good works are possible, real, and meritorious solely through God's grace and the infinite merits of Jesus Christ; but at the same time we are aware that, in virtue of possessing free will, we can accept or refuse the grace offered us by God; we can coöperate faithfully with it and put the talents given us out to usury, or we may receive grace in vain (2 Cor. vi, 1), and bury our talent in the earth. Hence we strive "by good works to make sure our calling and election" (2 Peter i, 10), and are convinced that if we neglect to do good works, we shall lose grace and fail to gain eternal life, but if we are zealous in their performance, we shall not only show our obedience but merit also a reward in heaven, for

St. Paul tells us that every man shall receive his own reward according to his labour (1 Cor. iii, 8), and our Lord Himself speaks of the joys of heaven as a reward. By our own exertions we could never gain this reward, and we feel how far all our works fall short of what God's grace purposes and is able to effect in us and by our agency. We know that we may well describe ourselves as unprofitable servants, but nevertheless when we faithfully coöperate voluntarily with God's grace, we are acting in conformity with His will and doing what is pleasing and meritorious in His sight. This is the teaching of divine revelation, and so far from supplying us with any ground for vainglory it impels us to serve God with thankful hearts, and to love Him who first loved us.

The Protestant doctrine appears to us most confused and out of harmony with Holy Scripture. It is quite a mistake to say that Catholicism teaches that sin can be completely removed by means of good works; the Church would repudiate such a doctrine, for she tells us that we are saved solely through faith in Christ and through His merits.

Luther maintained that by faith alone salvation was possible, such faith being independent of all good works and of charity, besides all that proceeds from charity. He believed man to be incapable of doing anything to please God, and considered.even our best actions to be sins. The Gospel, in Luther's opinion, tells us what Christ has done for men, not what it is the duty of men to do. A pious man sins in all his good works, and a good work performed in the best possible way is still a sin. Hence from one point of view Luther cried, "Away with all good works!" but on the other hand, he could not altogether ignore the explicit statements of Holy Scripture and the voice of conscience, so he opened a sort of backdoor to the good works that he had apparently discarded. According to the regulations for the Protestant Church in Württemberg good works ought to be performed in testimony of obedience and gratitude, and as the good fruits of penance, but not "with any idea that thereby we atone to God for our sins."

Surely it is impossible to reconcile these doctrines! How can there be good fruits where there is no good seed? Yet every seed of charity which might produce good works is to be absolutely excluded from the work of justification. And why should there be "good fruits of penance" where there is no thought of really making atonement for sin? Our Lord Himself compared a Christian working in God's service with men labouring in a vineyard (Matth. xx, 1–16); why did the labourers go to the vineyard if they did not expect to earn the stipulated wages?

For any one to assert that faith alone, exclusive of good works, can justify seems as unreasonable as it would be for a musician to say: "My talents and genius alone make me an artist; I can dispense with all my instruments, with my piano and violin, for my art does not reside in them; they are unnecessary or even injurious to it." It is, of course, true that he is an artist because he possesses certain natural gifts, and without them the most expensive piano in the world would not make him a musician. But still he must exercise his talents, he must study in order to develop them. He can neither retain nor display his powers unless he has an instrument and uses it with tireless industry. So is it with the life of a Christian. The ability to be a Christian comes to him solely through God's grace, and in order to preserve this ability he must have faith, which is as necessary to him as talent is to a musician, and is an unmerited gift of God just as much as an artistic genius is a gift. But the musician cannot develop and display his talent without an instrument, nor can a Christian develop and display his faith without good works.

The Commandments of God and of the Church

Protestants often say that with regard to good works there is a wide discrepancy between the teaching of the "better sort of Catholicism" and that of the papacy and its supporters. They acknowledge that much that is admirable may be found in the catechisms and devotional works of the Catholic Church, especially in the *Following of Christ*, but they maintain that the rules laid down by the Popes and the ordinary practices of the Church are very different. The commandments of God are treated as of secondary importance compared with those of the Church. Great stress is laid upon the observance of the prescribed holidays and upon attendance at Mass, which is said in Latin. The sermon is regarded as unimportant. There are, moreover, the so-called fast-days on which all kinds of dainties may be eaten and only flesh meat is forbidden. Great efficacy is ascribed to the repetition of certain forms of prayer, and this is a prominent part of the religious life. We very often read in papal documents that those who attend missions and make some sacrifice of money receive complete forgiveness for all their sins, etc. Such are the good works extolled and recommended by the papacy.

Statements such as the above enable us to see how difficult, how almost impossible, it is for people ignorant of our faith to understand our spiritual amd moral life. Where a Catholic recognizes harmony, they perceive nothing but jarring discords; a Catholic welcomes advice as tending to the salvation of his soul, or as revealing the will of God, to which he submits as willingly as a soldier to his officer's word of command, or a traveller to his guide's instructions, or a child to his parents' orders, but a non-Catholic talks about human legislation and oppressive constraint. When a soul, eager to be saved, asks the holy Catholic Church, "What must I do that I may have life everlasting?" it receives instruction and guidance. If it asks further, "The commandments I have kept from my youth, what is yet wanting to me?" the Church points out the higher way, that it may lay up treasure in heaven according to our Lord's words (Matth. xix, 21). The Church shows the sinner the path of penance, she stimulates all to unwearied zeal; she admonishes the holy to become yet more holy; for all she has some instruction, counsel, or command. She gives milk to babes and meat to the strong, and in all that she does and orders her only aim is to lead souls safely to Christ. But what advice or help can Protestantism supply to one desirous of attaining to perfection and salvation? Nothing but, "Believe, and do what you like; it is for you to order your own ways; only beware of believing or doing anything that might eventually lead you to Catholicism." This accounts for the restlessness of many dissatisfied souls, for their constant quest of fresh paths to salvation, and for their incessant search for new fountains after they have forsaken the old springs. It is false to say that there is a wide discrepancy between the teaching of the better sort of Catholicism and that of the papacy and its supporters. The *Following of Christ* is one of the fairest blossoms of Catholic moral theology, and no Pope has ever found fault with this book; on the contrary, all have agreed in recommending it as most useful in helping men to lead a good and truly Catholic life. The catechisms and books of devotion alluded to by Protestants were compiled by the supporters of the papacy and published with the sanction of the bishops. All alike teach most emphatically that the essence of Christian perfection and the way of salvation consist in loving God above all things and in following the example of our Lord Jesus Christ. There are other things which are more or less necessary means of attaining these ends, but they do not constitute perfection.

It is, therefore, equally untrue to say that the commandments of God are, in accordance with papal regulations, regarded as of secondary importance compared with those of the Church. If a music teacher tells his pupil to practise scales every day he does not imply that a musician's perfection consists in this exercise, but he considers that scales conduce to perfection and therefore he takes care that they shall not be neglected. If a physician orders a patient to refrain from certain kinds of food, no one is so foolish as to suppose that the physician cares less for his patient's health than for these directions. The rules and commandments of the Church, like God's commandments, serve the sole aim of training us to live as children of God and Holy Church, of promoting the welfare of our souls, and of guiding us to perfection. They are never the main thing, but are always only necessary means towards that end. A glance into any Catholic Catechism would suffice to convince any one that, in the moral instruction given to children, far more attention is paid to the commandments of God than to those of the Church.

We are certainly required to observe the holidays of obligation; but did not our Lord Himself observe the Jewish festivals? That assistance at Holy Mass is an essential part of the observance of a festival is a matter of course to any one who understands what the Mass is to Catholics, and who reads (Acts xx, 7) how, even in Apostolic days, Christians used to assemble not only to hear instructions but for the breaking of bread. St. Justin, who lived in the second century, tells us what they meant by this "breaking of bread." Protestants speak of Mass as being recited or performed, but most of it is read in a low voice, and Catholics follow in spirit even when they do not understand the Latin words. There is no lack of prayer books and devotional works, and the sermon is always in the vernacular. Protestants reproach us with regarding the latter as of little importance; the charge has been refuted many times but is constantly revived. The altar, and not the pulpit, is the central point in Catholic churches, but in every age the sermon has formed an important part of our worship, and the Council of Trent issued stringent orders that sermons should be preached on every Sunday and festival, and still more often, if necessary, in Lent and Advent. Moreover the faithful are to be admonished to hear the word of God expounded in their own parish church (sess. 24, cap. 4, can. 7 de ref.). Protestants object to our fast-days, and yet there is plenty of justification for them in the Bible (Joel ii, 12; Tob. xii, 8; Deut. ix, 18; Matth. xvii, 20; iv. 2; Acts xiv, 22). How they ought to be observed according to the spirit of the Church is taught in every catechism and by the life of almost any saint. No reference will be found there to all those dainties in which we are supposed to indulge on fast-days; and those who criticize our fasts, seem to have no idea of the distinction between fasting and abstinence from flesh meat.

Outward Practices

We are accused of attaching over great importance to the repetition of certain forms of prayer. Christ Himself ascribed the greatest possible power to prayer, and the *Our Father*, our Lord's own prayer, is the one most frequently used, although there is surely nothing un-Christian in using other forms of prayer or in preparing for the hour of death. It would undoubtedly be superstitious to ascribe any efficacy to the mere words, if they are uttered with no attention or devotion.

Some mention must be made of the old calumny that the Pope promises full forgiveness of all sins to such as subscribe to the so-called missions, etc. Even educated Protestants seem to believe that this is a fact, but not one Catholic, however ignorant, imagines any such absurdity.

Our antagonists display great ingenuity in representing our holy religion as a senseless medley of foolish outward practices and of rules made by men. They lay hold of some few points of Catholic observance, distort them, and then declare them to be the highly extolled good works that the Pope recommends. They are mistaken, however, and the fruits of the really good works in the Catholic Church may be seen by those who, impartially and without prejudice, study the lives of her saints. How many martyrs and confessors, missionaries and virgins, and servants of the sick and poor have sanctified themselves in every rank of life by means of poverty, self-sacrifice, humiliation, and labour, and have been brought by the Catholic Church to Jesus, the divine Shepherd of souls! Where are the fruits of Luther's famous doctrine that good works are impossible, useless, or even detrimental to salvation? Luther answers this question himself (second sermon on first Sunday of Advent): "As a result of this doctrine [that faith alone is necessary for salvation] the world as it grows older, grows more wicked, and people are now possessed by seven devils, whereas previously they were possessed by only one." On another occasion

(Wittenb., German ed., part 7, p. 241 b) he complained that the devil often reproached him with having taught what was wrong, and having disturbed the state of the churches, which under the papacy was calm and peaceful. "I cannot deny," he added, "that I am often filled with fear and anxiety." Those who had forsaken the ancient Church were finally compelled to abandon Luther's teaching on the subject of good works, and to return more or less to the Catholic doctrine that he had despised; life would otherwise have ceased to be possible. They were, however, very careful not to describe their changed opinions as Catholic, and so they took pains to misrepresent what the Catholic Church really taught. What Luther once said in another sense is perfectly true: "Unless the Pope fed us, as well as his own people, we should all die of hunger" (*Table Talk*, p. 269 a, Latin ed.).

The Evangelical Counsels

Protestants assert that in addition to requiring good works, the Catholic Church teaches that there are works of supererogation. If for instance any one goes into a monastery, he has, according to Roman Catholic opinion, abandoned the world, and secured assurance of salvation for others as well as himself, since, in taking the vows of religion, he does more than is actually demanded of him, and so lays up a store of merit which he does not need personally. Power is given to the Pope to use this treasury of the Church for the relief of the souls in purgatory.

In statements such as these it is hardly possible to recognize the truly biblical, Catholic doctrine regarding the evangelical counsels and their significance. Such a misrepresentation serves as a scarecrow to young Protestants, and is designed to prevent them from ever associating with people who believe in works of supererogation.

In speaking of Protestantism, Schopenhauer, who knew it intimately and was certainly not friendly to the Catholic Church, said that it had eliminated the central doctrine of Christianity and was gradually adopting the theory that a loving Father created the world for men's enjoyment, and if only they conform in some respects to His will, He intends to provide a much more beautiful world for them hereafter.

117

"This may be a good religion," adds Schopenhauer, "for well-to-do, married, and enlightened Protestant ministers, but it is not Christianity." Catholicism, on the contrary, requires each individual to be in earnest with regard to the strict obligations imposed by the Gospel. We know that there are various gifts and that what suits one, does not suit another. A man may be an excellent soldier and yet not be fit to command an army; another may be a first-rate farmer although he is a poor writer. Men differ in their tastes, talents, disposition, and vocation; and the Catholic moral law, which is based on the Bible, recognizes this fact. The Church teaches that all are called to perfection, and are bound to strive after it as long as they live (Matth. v, 48). Each, however, ought to be perfect in his own state of life. Some can exclaim with St. Paul, "The charity of Christ presseth us" (2 Cor. v, 14), and these follow the Apostle's admonition and seek the better gifts of grace and more perfect charity (1 Cor. xii, 31, and xiii), asking with the rich young man, "Master, what good shall I do, that I may have life everlasting?" If such as these receive the answer, "Keep the commandments," they are not satisfied, but ask again, "What is yet wanting to me?" They long to do more than their bounden duty. Slavish souls work only under compulsion; a bureaucrat's life is regulated by formal precepts and he is contented to do his ordinary routine, but even in secular callings there are many who do far more than is strictly required of them. Human society bestows on such men orders and distinctions, monuments are erected in their honour, and their names are recorded in history. In the Church of Christ, too, the Holy Ghost impels many favoured souls to higher efforts, and inspires them with the desire to do, sacrifice, and suffer everything for love of Christ and for the salvation of souls, — their own, primarily, but also those of others, that thus they may win all for Christ. Can it be expected of Holy Church that she should treat these children of hers as Luther would have her do? He declared that whoever maintained good works and vows to be efficacious, was under the influence of the devil and false to the faith (Wittenb., vi, 200 b), and warned people not to be too good: "Why should we worry ourselves with the attempt to make men pious?" (*Table Talk*, Latin ed., 290, and ed. Aurifaber, 178.) According to Luther the Church ought not to describe as perfect a life wholly dedicated to the service of God, nor ought she to call those who desire to lead such a life "her joy and her crown." Would any king treat his most loyal and devoted servants thus? About fourteen hundred years ago Salvianus made a remark that still holds good: "Hatred against the religious orders increases in proportion to the decay of religion among the nations."

Why does any Catholic enter a monastery? Not in order to obtain perfect certainty of salvation, for many may go to perdition in spite of having worn the religious habit. Still less does he fancy that he will have nothing to do but lead an easy existence within the monastery walls, paying a merely external obedience to the rules of the Order; such a life would be no better than life out in the world. Nor does he dream of being able henceforth to sell his works of supererogation. What pitiful little minds those people must possess who can invent such charges! No; a Catholic enters a monastery in order to serve God with the greatest possible application, in accordance with his own vocation and inclinations, to tread most faithfully the narrow way that leads to heaven, to bear his cross, to deny himself, and to follow Christ who had not where to lay His head, who lived a pure and celibate life, and for our sake became obedient even unto death.

How does he pass his time in the monastery? In voluntary poverty, for our Saviour said to the rich young man, "If thou wilt be perfect, go, sell what thou hast and give to the poor . . . and come, follow me" (Matth. xix, 21). He leads a chaste and frugal life, for Christ said, "There are eunuchs, who have made themselves eunuchs for the kingdom of heaven; he that can take, let him take it" (Matth. xix, 12), and St. Paul wrote, "I would that all men were even as myself [i.e., unmarried] . . . Concerning virgins, I have no commandment of the Lord, but I give counsel," etc. (see 1

Cor. vii). Finally every one in a monastery has to deny himself and practise absolute obedience to his spiritual superior, thus becoming like Him who came, not to do His own will, but the will of Him that sent Him. A soldier swears to be loyal to his king, and in the same way, after an adequate probation, a religious binds himself voluntarily by solemn vows to serve God and observe these three evangelical counsels.

It is enough to mention the Orders founded respectively by St. Benedict and St. Francis, and the work done by St. Vincent de Paul, for my readers to acknowledge at once that the Church, civilization, and human society in general all owe them a great debt of gratitude. Can a root be bad that produces such charming and luxurious blossoms of virtue and purity, such precious fruits of charity, designed to alleviate every imaginable form of suffering? It is indeed true that the innumerable servants and handmaids of Christ, who have devoted all their time and faculties to following their divine Master's example, have obtained salvation for many besides themselves and have stored up a wealth of merit in which others participate. But neither they nor the Church bargain and trade with their good works. They coöperate loyally with the graces that come to them through Christ's merits alone, and they transmit them freely to others. They are like a fertile field that produces, for the support of the needy, the fruits that the sun has ripened.

The late Vice-President Sherman, addressing the graduating class at Nazareth, Michigan, May 18, 1911, said in part:

"To me the Catholic Sisterhood seems to be one of the strongest proofs of the existence of a hereafter. I speak not as a member of the Catholic Church, or a sectarian, or a member of any religious belief. These noble women have given up all that they have in this world, their wealth, their homes, their friends, their hearts, their lives, and have devoted all their energies and entire attention to the rearing of others' children, to the guiding of youths and to the turning of mature minds to loftier sentiments with no hope whatever of any reward, except that which they hope for in the great beyond.

"There is no more potent demonstration of the existence of God than the work of the Sisters. All praise, all honor to the great army of the Catholic Sisterhoods!"

Lina Eckenstein, in the preface to her work on *Woman Under Monasticism*, says: "The attitude of mind which had been harbored and cultivated in the cloister, must be reckoned among the most civilizing influences which have helped to develop mental and moral strength in Western Europe."

Self-Righteousness

Protestants proceed to say, further, that the ease with which Catholics can do penance and make satisfaction, in conjunction with their lamentable theory regarding works of supererogation, gives rise on the one hand to a frivolous spirit that takes God's commandments and their fulfilment far too lightly, and, on the other hand, to a self-righteous arrogance that relies for salvation upon good works of one's own selection.

A statement such as this makes one wonder whether Protestants ever read the lives of Catholic saints. No one who had ever done so could produce such a distorted misrepresentation of Catholic life and activity. What saint or preacher ever taught that we might take God's commandments and their fulfilment lightly? Did any saint ever live in self-righteous arrogance, relying upon good works of his own selection? An examination of the whole *Acta Sanctorum* would not result in the discovery of a single saint of this kind. There are, unhappily, Catholics who take God's commandments lightly, but even they would hardly imagine themselves to be on the right road on this account, and it is certain that Catholicism combats, rather than encourages, self-righteous arrogance. Professor Harnack, a Protestant theologian, bears the following testimony to our Church: "Confidence in God, unfeigned humility, certainty of salvation, and devotion to the service of the brethren are all to be found in the Catholic Church; numerous brethren take up the cross of Christ and through the practice of self-condemnation attain to joy in God, such as Paul and Augustine experienced."

It is strange that Protestants are unable to believe in the existence of really moral virtue and greatness apart from self-righteousness, and cannot see that striving after perfection is the necessary condition of all religious life, whereas to fancy oneself to have reached the climax of perfection would be to deal it its deathblow.

It is in the Bible that we find the good works enumerated to which God promises a glorious reward; yet we have been bitterly reproached for discovering in Holy Scripture anything about duties and rewards. It is a strange fact that the people who used to cry, "Down with your false and evil doctrine of good works, whereby you flatter yourselves that you can please God; we glory only in the justice of Christ," — these very people now boast of possessing what they once abused us for having. They must not take it too much amiss if we prefer to adhere to the old Catholic teaching and refrain from adopting the new Protestant theory.

To a Catholic the good works recommended in Luther's Catechism — for we may disregard his other works — are of a rather startling character. For instance, the following passage occurs in his Longer Catechism: "When nature, as implanted in us by God, impels us and is resisted, it is impossible to live chastely in a state of celibacy." It may be true enough that we are poor miserable Christians, subject to the ordinances of men, and so blinded as to need many prayers. No one can fail to benefit by prayers offered with a good intention, but it is hardly likely that our Protestant fellow Christians pray much for us; nor do they follow Luther's admonition, uttered on his deathbed: "Pray for our Lord God (!) and His Gospel, that it may be well with Him, for the Council of Trent and the Pope himself are angry with Him" (*Historie und Predigt des Cölius zu Eisleben*, 1546). Protestants are more disposed to abuse and hate us than to pray for us; for instance, in Luther's "prayer" (*Sämtl. Werke*, Erl., xxv, 107) occur the words, "If I am to say, ' Hallowed be

Thy Name,' I must add, 'Accursed, damned, and dishonoured be the names of papists.' If I am to say, 'Thy kingdom come,' I must add, 'Accursed, damned, and destroyed be the papacy.' This is the prayer that I offer unceasingly with heart and voice every day."

It must be acknowledged, moreover, that this proposal to pray for us savours somewhat of the prayer mentioned in Luke xviii, 11. We poor publicans are first abused as blind and deluded people who fancy ourselves able to help others by our works of supererogation, and in the same breath our opponents tell us that they propose to help us by means of intercessory prayer on our behalf, such prayer being a work of supererogation!

VI. THE VENERATION OF SAINTS

The Protestant Assertion. According to Roman Catholic doctrine, it is a duty to invoke the saints, to have recourse to their help and intercession, to regard their relics as sacred, and to show suitable honour to their statues and pictures. Roman Catholics are taught to rely particularly upon the Mother of Jesus Christ, who is called the Queen of Heaven and Ruler of the World, and who is believed to have been, from her birth onwards, uncontaminated with original sin. It is a duty to kneel in prayer to this Queen of Heaven and to others, whom the Catholic Church has raised to the dignity of saints, and to expect help and the cure of disease at places where their relics are preserved, or even from miraculous medals and statues of Mary.

The Catholic Reply. 1. The Catholic Church does not teach that we *must* invoke the saints, but only that we *may* do so, and that it is a good and beneficial practice, because we rely upon reason and Holy Scripture and believe that the saints take an interest in their brethren here on earth (Luke xv, 10) and pray for them (2 Mach. xv, 14). 2. As to the Mother of Jesus Christ, whom we are supposed to worship as a divine person and as our only Redeemer, we are indeed taught to put great confidence in her, but we rely chiefly on her divine Son. We trust that Mary, the much loved Mother of God, will intercede for us, but we know that Jesus alone can save us. 3. If the Apostles of Christ are to be rulers and judges in His kingdom, without detriment to His honour, there can be no harm in calling the Mother of our heavenly King Queen and ruler of heaven; we do so in a childlike spirit of reverence, and every Catholic understands what is meant. 4. That Mary was conceived without original sin is only the necessary result of her position in the scheme of our redemption. The contrary opinion has never prevailed among Christians. 5. The Catholic Church does not raise the dead to the dignity of saints, but, after a long and careful investigation, she allows us to venerate as holy some of her members whom God Himself has sanctified. 6. With regard to statues and pictures, the Council of Trent decided that due honour should be shown them; not that we believe there to be anything divine about them, nor that we ought to rely upon them, but simply because in honouring them we worship Christ and testify our reverence for the saints.

Charles Kingsley wrote: "Why should not those who are gone to the Lord be actually nearerus, not farther from us, in the heavenly world; praying for us, and it may be influencing and guiding us in a hundred ways, of which we, in our prison-house of mortality, can not dream?" (*Letters and Memories*, II, 264).

According to Protestant Doctrine it is proper to respect the memory of good and holy persons, and especially of our Lord's Mother; we may consider how they died and imitate their faith, but nowhere in Holy Scripture are we told to address any petition to a departed saint; we ought rather to have recourse to Jesus Christ, the one Mediator between God and man (1 Tim. ii, 5), who is able to hear us and promises that He will not cast out those who come to Him (John vi, 37).

The Catholic Reply. The first part of the preceding paragraph states the Catholic practice with regard to the saints. If in addition to honouring them we ask their intercession, we do so in reliance upon the words of Holy Scripture, where we read that "the continual prayer of a just man availeth much" (James v, 16). St. Paul had no intention of denying that Christ was the only Mediator between God and man when he asked his converts to pray for him (e.g., 1 Thess. v, 25), nor has the Catholic who now asks some saint to intercede for him any idea of denying it. He distrusts his own worthiness, but not God's omnipotence and mercy.

COMMENTARY

The Catholic doctrine on the subject of invocation of the saints is said to encourage their worship, which is detrimental to God's glory and to that of our only Mediator, Jesus Christ.

Hence the explicit statement made by the Council of Trent, and reproduced in all Catholic books of instruction, is assumed to have no weight. As a matter of fact, the veneration that we pay to the saints, and especially to the dear Mother of God, ought to lead us to Christ and not away from Him. The saints are the choicest fruits of His redeeming Blood; they are His friends and loyal servants; and now in heaven they love their fellow servants as ardently as they did on earth. Hence we honour them and ask their prayers, knowing well that both our reverence for them and their intercession for us are results of the reconciliation effected by Jesus Christ who unites all the redeemed in the bond of brotherhood. This is why in all her prayers, even when she invokes the intercession of the saints, the Church invariably turns to God Himself, and concludes with the words, "Through Jesus Christ our Lord." Protestants would have to lay aside one of their most effectual weapons against us, were they to recognize the truth on this subject, and perceive that the Catholic Church honours, loves, and adores Jesus Christ as the one Mediator, whereas by many Protestants, even by preachers and professors, He is now no longer regarded as divine, and is hardly honoured as a saint. This fact is enough to prove that the veneration of saints, practised in the Catholic Church, has not, in the course of nineteen centuries, led that Church away from Christ. Worthy Protestants are not allowed to know all this, and over and over again, in Sunday schools and from the pulpit, they are told that we Catholics deprive Christ of the honour due to Him, that we worship idols and pray to the saints and to Mary. Very few converts to Catholicism escape having remarks of this kind thrust upon them.

Dr. Schaff says: "To say that Papists are idolators is a colossal slander on the oldest and largest Church in Christendom, and is untrue, unjust, uncharitable and unchristian" (*Creed Revisions*, p. 36).

The Veneration of Mary

Protestants maintain that in invoking Mary we infringe upon the honour of God. In the Roman Breviary Mary is addressed thus: "Thou art the only hope of sinners, through thee we hope for forgiveness of our offences, in thee we have the fullest hope of reward.'' (The beautiful old hymn *Ave Maris stella* is quoted in support of the Protestant charges, in spite of its containing the words: *Sumat per te preces, Qui pro nobis natus, Tulit esse tuus.*) Moreover Catholics speak of Mary as "Queen of all creatures," "Eternal source of healing," "Refuge for all who have recourse to her." A Roman Catholic priest must suggest to a dying man the following ejaculations: "Into Thy hands I commend my spirit; Lord Jesus, receive my soul. Holy Mary, pray for me; Mary, Mother of grace and Mother of mercy, do thou defend me from the enemy, and receive me at the hour of death."

Ever since the time of the Council of Trent, Mariolatry has been increasing and culminated under Pius IX who declared: "Our salvation rests upon the holy Virgin, since God deposited in her all the fulness of good, so that, if any hope and any spiritual healing exist for us, we receive them solely and alone from her." A Protestant, hearing these words, asks with a sigh what has become of our Saviour.

We, who still believe in our Saviour, feel inclined to ask in our turn, "From whom did we receive Him? From whom have we derived all our information regarding His wonderful conception and birth? Was it not from her through whom our heavenly Father bestowed Him upon us sinners? He rested on the lap of His virgin Mother both in the stable at Bethlehem and at the foot of the cross." We might almost go so far as to ask, "What becomes of our Saviour among those who refuse to honour Mary as the virgin Mother of God? Does He not lose, in consequence of their refusal, the divine honour that is His due?" In hymns and the pious effusions of devout souls, it is true that expressions occur which must be understood according to the spirit in which they are written, but in the Roman Breviary and Missal there is not a single prayer addressed to any saint or to the Blessed Virgin personally. All are addressed to God, and all are petitions for the graces which Christ alone merited on our behalf. For instance, the prayer said at the Angelus is: "Pour forth, O Lord, Thy grace into our hearts, that we, to whom the incarnation of Christ Thy Son was made known by the message of an angel, may, by His Passion and Cross, be brought to the glory of His resurrection, through the same Christ our Lord." On the feast of the Immaculate Conception the Church prays: "O God, who by the Virgin's Immaculate Conception didst prepare a worthy dwelling for Thy Son, we beseech Thee, that Thou, who by the death of that same Son of Thine, foreseen by Thee, didst preserve her from every stain, wouldst grant that by her intercession we also may be purified, and so come to Thee. Through the same Jesus Christ our Lord." This is the prayer used on a great festival in honour of our Lady, and throughout it refers to Christ; how is it then possible to ask, "What has become of our Saviour?"

We are told that ever since the time of the Council of Trent Mariolatry has been increasing, and culminated under Pius IX. Protestants ought to realize that Mariolatry began with the angel's salutation, and cannot rise to any higher point than was reached when God, in His gracious design, chose Mary to be the Mother of our Lord. It is worth while perhaps to quote what Luther says in his exposition of the *Magnificat:* "These great things were that Mary had become Mother of God, and when this took place so many great favours were conferred upon her that no one can understand them. For there resulted from it all the honour and glory that she alone of the whole human race is exalted above all others [may we not call such a person "Queen" over all the rest?] and none is equal to her, and that she has one Son in common with our heavenly Father, and such a Son! When we speak of her as Mother of God, no one could say anything greater of her or to her, not though he had as many tongues as there are leaves and blades of grass, stars in heaven and grains of sand on the seashore."

Preaching in the Collegiate Baptist Church in New York, in 1912, Rev. Dr. Oscar Haywood said that there had been mischievous reactions in religious thought since the Reformation. "One of those," he said, "has resulted in the creation of a prejudice with respect to the Holy Virgin. Her name is rarely mentioned in a Protestant Church. We have dispossessed her of that honour and glory which is hers by divine right."

The *Western Christian Advocate* (Methodist) likewise deplores this dethronement of Mary: "We cannot recall ever having heard a sermon preached from our Protestant pulpits upon the character of Mary, and the subject would seem almost to be tabooed, lest the preacher be misunderstood. Mary of Nazareth is scarcely mentioned even in any list of the world's greatest women, and yet she gave birth to the world's Redeemer, watched over His infancy, trained Him in boyhood when He was subject to His parents, and it was in her home that Jesus lived. . . . Why should not Protestants, then, look upon her as a type and representative of the highest and holiest womanhood?"

Long centuries before the Council of Trent, the liturgy of St. James was in use in Jerusalem, and it contained the following prayer uttered by the priest: "O Mother of our Lord Jesus Christ, intercede for me with thine only Son, that He may pardon my sins, and accept this sacrifice offered by my sinful hands." The Fathers of the Church vie with one another in honouring the Mother of God, and the invocations in the Breviary, to which Protestants object so strongly, are extremely ancient. In the name of all the bishops assembled at the Council of Ephesus in 431, St. Cyril addressed a prayer to our Lady, in which he called her "the venerable jewel of the whole world, the support of the true faith, the firm foundation of all churches, the Mother of God, through whom the entire universe attains to a knowledge of the truth," etc. St. Bernard gives a beautiful explanation of our reason for calling Mary the Star of the Sea.

How deep, tender, and true is our love of Mary! In her honour poetry has produced its choicest blossoms and art its masterpieces. We shall never allow carping criticism to diminish our devotion to her, for we are convinced that those who attempt to rob us of Mary the Mother, would in the end deprive us also of Christ her divine Son. St. Bernard was never weary of praising our Lady, but did he on that account think little of our Lord? No, it was he who extolled the sacred Name of Jesus in the sweetest strains. St. Athanasius stands almost unrivalled in his triumphant defence of the divinity of Christ by word of mouth and in writing, amidst indescribable sufferings, and his love and enthusiasm for our Saviour were not diminished by his profound reverence for the Mother of God. All the great doctors, saints, and heroes of antiquity loved and praised, honoured and invoked Mary the immaculate Mother, but they did not therefore forget Christ. It would be well if at the present day our Saviour were known, loved, and served as He was in the past by those who reverenced His dear Mother most deeply. Protestants need not ask us what has become of our Saviour; we are in good company and on the right path whenever we say an *Ave Maria.*

John Ruskin was sensible of the gracious influence of "the Madonna" on the lives and characters of women: "I am persuaded that the worship of the Madonna has been one of the noblest and most vital graces, and has never been otherwise than productive of true holiness of life and purity of character" (*Fors Clavigera*, II, Letter XLI).

The Immaculate Conception

We are told further that Pius IX raised the theory of our Lady's Immaculate Conception to the rank of a dogma of the Catholic Church, but travellers to Rome, even during the reign of his predecessor, had opportunity to convince themselves that festivals in honour of Mary were observed with as much or even more splendour and solemnity as the greatest Christian holidays.

The contrast emphasized in this statement is rather obscure. Of course festivals in honour of our Lady were observed in Rome before 1854; they were observed even more than a thousand years before that date. It is certain that the feast of the Annunciation was observed in 656 as "the feast of the Blessed Virgin," and it is highly probable that the feast of the Immaculate Conception was celebrated about that period (Martène, *de antiq. eccl. rit.*, III, 557). It is also true that in Rome festivals are observed with more splendour than the greatest Christian festivals in Protestant churches. Do Protestants suppose that on such occasions Catholics never think of Christ, and kneel in adoration of Mary alone? If a Protestant, who abhors every kind of Catholic festival, asserts that feasts of our Lady were observed in Rome during the reign of Pius IX's predecessor with even more splendour than the greatest Christian holidays, such an assertion leads to nothing, although it may perhaps intensify the belief, carefully fostered in young Protestants, that Roman Catholics are idolaters.

On December 8, 1854, amidst the enthusiastic applause of the Catholic Church, the dogma of the Immaculate Conception was solemnly defined by Pius IX, who proclaimed as a revealed truth, consistent with Holy Scripture and tradition, what had previously been only a matter of pious belief, although long investigations had resulted in establishing its truth, and Catholics had at all times felt that any contrary opinion was untenable. The definition of this dogma did not cause any Catholic to waver in his faith in Christ as our only Mediator, nor did it make any one rely less upon our Lord's merits. So far from this dogma being derogatory to the honour of Christ, it increases the glory of Him who, by His precious Blood alone, purchased this signal favour for His Mother. Ten years after his revolt against the Church, Luther still believed in the Immaculate Conception of Mary, for he wrote: "Other human beings are conceived in sin, but Mary was conceived full of grace. The angel could not have said, 'Blessed art thou,' if she had ever lain under the curse" (Walch, II, 2616).

If in any place veneration of the saints is put on a level with the service of God, and if the homage due to God alone is offered to a saint, this is not the result of the Catholic faith but in direct opposition to it; and to condemn such practices is right and praiseworthy. They do not occur, however, among properly instructed Catholics.

Relics of the Saints

With regard to the veneration of relics Protestants remind us that their genuineness is often called in question, as in the case of the Holy

Coat. Yet it is notorious that people come in thousands to visit such relics, especially at the times when special indulgences are granted to pilgrims.

People are always fond of honouring the memory of great and popular persons. They reverence Luther's Bible, for which the Emperor Leopold paid one hundred and fify pounds in order to display his partiality for the Lutheran party. But we are discussing the relics of Christians who were remarkable for sanctity displayed in the service of God; we need not concern ourselves with Lutheran relics. We read in one of the earliest Christian records, the account of the martyrdom of St. Ignatius (about 110. A.D.), that the saint's bones were wrapped in linen and preserved as a priceless treasure. St. Augustine tells us of many miracles that took place at the tombs of the martyrs, and similar marvels have recurred in every age of the Church. In the Bible we read that contact with the bones of Eliseus restored a dead man to life (4 Kings xiii, 21), and that when handkerchiefs and aprons belonging to St. Paul were brought to the sick, their diseases departed from them (Acts xix, 12). St. Peter's very shadow delivered the sick from their infirmities (Acts v, 15), and Luther himself asked, "Who can challenge the fact that God works miracles through the names of His saints?" (*Unterricht*, Wittenb. ed., VII, 7 b.)

The editor of the Methodist periodical, the *Christian Herald*, tells a correspondent (Dec. 20, 1911) that "to assume that the day of miracles is past, would be to assume that the Divine power is shortened."

We know of course that some relics are spurious or of doubtful authenticity, but this no more affects the veneration of relics than the fact that there is bad money interferes with the circulation of good coin.

Protestants say that the common popular belief ascribes to relics, and to miraculous representations of our Lady, the same sort of power as the ancient Greeks and Romans ascribed to the statues of their gods. The Council of Trent forbade any one to assume that statues and pictures possess miraculous powers, but the authorities of the Catholic Church allow pilgrimages to statues of Mary in churches under their control. More than once eminent men in the Catholic Church, on hearing of miracles ascribed to such figures, have suggested, though unsuccessfully, that there might be some coöperation of diabolical forces. Nevertheless, the Popes have invariably taken churches containing such statues under their protection, and have gone so far at least as to say that the holy Mother of God permits her wonders to be seen there. Finally we are told that weeping, moving, and miraculous statues continue to attract the poor and ignorant whose pastors fail to warn them against such things, and thousands still make pilgrimages in order to pray to them.

We may perhaps express our regret that poor ignorant Protestants still continue to be encouraged by their pastors to look upon Catholics, not merely as idolaters but actually as devil-worshippers. Eminent Catholics have suggested — or so it is said — that the devil haunts places of pilgrimage, making statues of our Lady move and weep, and even working miracles in front of them. Yet we bend the knee before him and adore him present in the statues; we may not realize what we are doing, but we are practically acting like the pagans of old. Protestants persist in saying that the statue of our Lady at Einsiedeln can be set in motion by means of wires; the statement may be disproved a thousand times, but still they believe it.

The great French preacher Bourdaloue (*Pensées div. sur la foi*) speaks of people who oppose religion by raising objections of this kind, continually copying and repeating the charges brought forward by others, and imagining that their assertions will effect our downfall. Such people show, he says, their inability to venture upon a serious attack on religion. Some point of no importance, not affecting our religion as a whole, is singled out for attack; it may be some devotional exercise, some ceremony, or custom that attracts their notice, and that might and would be altered at once if it really endangered our faith in God and our hope in our Redeemer. Against this comparative trifle they expend all their efforts and eloquence. Our religion undoubtedly rests on a sure foundation, since men dare to attack it only from a safe distance.

The Catholic doctrine regarding statues and pictures and the honour paid to them was enunciated very clearly by the

Council of Trent, which forbade us to believe that there is in them anything divine, or any force for the sake of which we venerate them. The Council ordered us not to expect favours from them nor to rely on them, but to give all the honour to those whom they represent. This is the doctrine of the Catholic Church. Where are the weeping, moving, and wonder-working statues? Has any one ever seen them? Protestants accuse us of going in hundreds of thousands to visit them, but we Catholics should be at a loss to say where one such statue exists.

Pilgrimages

Pilgrimages are not ordered by the Church, but are the outcome of a sentiment common to mankind, and may be productive of much good if they are performed in a proper spirit.

It is a fact that there are places privileged by nature, and possessing health-giving waters and a salubrious climate. It is also a fact that there are places that exercise a kind of spiritual attraction, so that a Christian believes that he can pray there better than elsewhere, either because he can contemplate some venerable picture, or because he will enjoy unusual calm and opportunity for recollection, or because he will find there some experienced counsellor to advise him.

Do not lovers of art make pilgrimages to places where their artistic sense is stimulated and gratified? Has not the house formerly occupied by some great poet power to attract his admirers? Why may not Catholics be allowed to seek spiritual refreshment at their places of pilgrimage? And why cannot the authorities be trusted to take care that this ancient Christian custom does not degenerate into superstition? Whether Protestants believe it or not, God alone is the object of all worship at our places of pilgrimage, and it is scandalous that those, who profess to be Christians like ourselves, should speak of Catholics as idolaters.

What does Luther say of the part played by the devil in his own work? He tells us that he licked more than one block of salt with the devil (Sermon, "Reminiscence"), and that the devil slept with him more frequently than his wife (*Table Talk*, f. 158). He learned how to abolish the holy Sacrifice of the Mass from no one but the devil himself (Op. Jen., VI, f. 82). When the devil reproached him with his sins, Luther sent him away, saying, "My dear devil, pray for me, and others in similar temptations shall also say, 'Holy devil, pray for us'" (*Table·Talk*, 286, 287, Frankf., f. 289, 292). In one short work written against the Duke of Brunswick, Luther mentions the devil one hundred and forty-six times.

Finally, before leaving the subject, we may perhaps point out that many who object to our veneration of saints are impelled to do so, not so much by zeal for Christ's honour as by a kind of jealousy due to the fact that Protestantism produces no saints. Lavater, one of the shining lights of the Protestant Church, in writing to L. von Stolberg, a convert to Catholicism, says: "You have saints, I admit, and we have none, or at least none like yours." Gregorovius, a famous Protestant historian, says (*Röm. Tagebuch*): "They stand in admiration before those giants of Catholicism, the saints, but they do not ask how it comes to pass that Protestantism produces none. They suspect the mysterious depth and force of Catholicism, but they are afraid to come too near it; and so they pass it by with a timid and wistful glance. They gloat over the ages of decadence, for then they can look shocked as they speak of the corruption of the papacy, for nothing of the sort occurs in their midst. From the height of their shallow and pitiful moralism, devoid of all strength and stability, they pronounce their charitable judgment in which as a rule they declare that they will be quite satisfied and at ease, if only the Church is completely destroyed."

VII. THE SACRAMENTS

The Protestant Assertion. With regard to the Holy Eucharist, Protestants differ from Catholics on three important points, and condemn the papal doctrines on the subject of: transubstantiation, the Sacrifice of the Mass, and Communion in one kind.

The Catholic Reply. These are not merely papal doctrines that are condemned by Protestants, but the plain teaching of Jesus Christ Himself to which all Christians adhered prior to the Reformation. The Reformers substituted their own human views and doctrines, that are in many cases contradictory, for the word of God is handed down from antiquity. The Catholic Church simply accepts our Lord's words, "This is my Body," whereas Protestants assign all sorts of artificial meanings to them.

The Protestant Assertion. The Roman Catholic Church teaches with regard to transubstantiation that when the priest utters the words of consecration over the host and the chalice, the bread and wine are changed into the Body and Blood of Jesus Christ, so that their substance is completely altered. This change is called transubstantiation; it accounts for the care and reverence displayed in touching the consecrated host.

The Catholic Reply. The Catholic Church simply accepts our Lord's words, "This is my Body." She believes that by His almighty word Christ changed the bread into His holy Body and the wine into His holy Blood, and that He gave His Apostles power to do the same. Hence, when we adore the Blessed Sacrament, we certainly do not worship bread but Christ, who is truly, really, and substantially present under the species of bread.

The Protestant Churches teach, on the other hand, that at Holy Communion the true Body and Blood of Christ are received together with the bread and wine, as St. Paul says in 1 Cor. x, 16. Therefore in Holy Communion the bread and wine are not mere appearances, deceiving the senses, but they are true, visible signs with which the invisible gift of the Body and Blood of Christ is bestowed. If we receive them with contrite and believing hearts, we obtain remission of sins and everlasting life (Matth. xxvi, 28; John vi, 51, 54).

The Catholic Reply. As Christ did not say, "This bread is my Body," we cannot believe that what He held in His hands after saying "This is my Body" was still bread, but it was truly His Body under the form of bread. Luther's interpretation is contrary to the words of Holy Scripture, and to the belief of all Christendom before his time. St. Paul's words in 1 Cor. x do not admit of any other interpretation than that assigned to them by all Christians unanimously during the first fifteen centuries of the Church's existence. It is not the wine but the chalice that St. Paul calls "the communion of the blood of Christ." When he says that the bread which we break is the partaking of the Body of the Lord, he means the food that we receive; he does not mean that the substance of bread is still really present. In the same way the Catholic Church calls the consecrated host "bread of heaven," without meaning that it is really still bread.

With regard to the Sacrifice of the Mass, Protestants think that the doctrine of the Catholic Church is this: When the priest, by uttering the words of consecration, has effected the transubstantiation of the bread and wine into the Body and Blood of Christ, he can offer them daily to God as an atoning sacrifice, and thus obtain forgiveness of sin both for the living and for the souls in purgatory.

The Catholic Reply. No, the Church does not teach that the priest can sacrifice the bread to God after transubstantiation has taken place. The Catholic doctrine is that the priest at the altar does precisely what Christ did in the Cenaculum, and what He ordered His Apostles to do, viz., he pronounces the words of consecration that effect transubstantiation, he offers a sacrifice and at the same time he prepares food for our souls.

Protestants often make the following assertion: We read in the New Testament of thank offerings which all Christians, being a priestly nation, ought to make to Almighty God; but we read of only *one* atoning sacrifice, offered by our Lord when He died on the Cross (Hebr. ix, 28). This sacrifice was made once for all, and therefore there is no need of any other, "for by one oblation He hath perfected for ever them that are sanctified" (Hebr. x, 14). Hence we cannot admit that there is any other sacrifice offered in the Church.

The Catholic Reply. The Catholic Church has not instituted another new sacrifice over and above the one atoning sacrifice offered by Jesus Christ, but she carries out His instructions and continues His work as she has done ever since the time of the Apostles. Sacrifice is an essential part of this work, and we read that the Church of the New Testament also possesses an altar (Hebr. xiii, 10). Luther and his followers abolished the offering of Holy Mass, but their action does not affect the Catholic Church, and she continues to offer it because Christ ordered her to do so and according to His institution (cf. Luke xxii, 19).

Protestants believe that the Catholic rule regarding the administration of Holy Communion is that the officiating priest may drink the consecrated wine but may not give it to the laity.

The Catholic Reply. All that the Catholic Church teaches on the subject is that the laity, and also priests who are not offering the holy sacrifice, are not bound by any divine obligation to communicate under both kinds. As Christ is present, whole and undivided, under one species, he who receives under one kind only is not deprived of any grace necessary to salvation. The rule that Holy Communion should be administered only under the form of bread was laid down by the Catholic Church for practical reasons, and might be altered, provided that the faith in the Real Presence of Christ remained unaffected.

Protestants argue that at the Last Supper our Lord said, "Drink ye *all* of this," hence they feel bound to adhere to this rule, believing that thus only they can receive the full benefit of this holy feast. The early Christians used to receive the chalice, and it was only by an unwarrantable exercise of power and after many struggles that the Popes deprived the laity of this privilege.

The Catholic Reply. Our Lord's words were addressed only to the Apostles. Both our Saviour Himself (John vi) and St. Paul (1 Cor. xi, 27) ascribed the beneficial effect of the Holy Sacrament to eating the Lord's Body alone. The early Christians were undoubtedly accustomed to receive the consecrated chalice, but they did not believe that thus only they could enjoy the full benefit of the sacrament. Conflicts arose, not because Catholics protested against being deprived of the chalice by the Popes, but because some people made the withholding of the chalice a pretext for their rebellion against the Church.

COMMENTARY

The teaching of the Catholic Church on the subject of the Sacrifice of the Mass and the transubstantiation that takes place during it, is fully in harmony with Holy Scripture and with oral tradition. Jesus Christ Himself spoke of His Body as given or sacrificed and of His Blood as shed for sinners. Hence even at the Last Supper He offered a true sacrifice in the Holy Sacrament. The Apostles taught that this was so, and there is still extant a work dating from the first or second century in which there is an allusion to the sacrifice on the Lord's day; cf. also St. Cyril of Alexandria and others. We still have sacrificial prayers dating from the earliest ages of Christianity, and in no Church before Luther's was the sacrifice ever denied, nor is there any record of any one having newly introduced the Sacrifice of the Mass. We are in complete conformity with the will of Christ, as it was understood and carried out by the Apostles.

The holy Sacrifice of the Mass cannot detract from the merit of the Sacrifice of the Cross because the two sacrifices are essentially the same. The words of a preacher do not detract from the words of Christ, the sole Teacher of truth, for a preacher who is commissioned by Christ and teaches in His spirit, proclaims the same doctrine as Christ proclaimed on earth, which can reach us only through the agency of men. In the same way the sacrifice offered by the priest in the name and by the authority of Christ, brings vividly before us, children of a later age, the sacrifice offered by Christ, and the channel of graces once merited by Him is opened to us afresh every day. No Catholic has ever believed or taught that even the smallest grace for either the living or the dead is merited by the priest's actions at the altar of themselves. It is through the priest's agency that the words of Christ reach each individual in his congregation, and yet Christ remains the way, the truth, and the life; similarly it is also through the priest's agency that the one great atoning sacrifice of the New Testament, with all its wealth of grace, is brought into contact with individuals, although Christ is still the one high priest and the perfect sacrifice. We preach no other doctrine than Christ crucified, and we offer no other sacrifice than Christ, to the Jews a stumbling block and to the Gentiles folly.

Sacraments and Blessings

Protestantism teaches that Christ instituted two sacraments, Baptism and the Lord's Supper, in which He bestows on us invisible heavenly gifts together with the visible signs. The Catholic Church, according to Protestants, looks upon sacraments in another light, and since the year 1439 she has reckoned seven sacraments, as well as various forms of blessing (*benedictiones*) to which scarcely less efficacy is ascribed than to the sacraments themselves. The importance of Baptism and the Lord's Supper is not sufficiently emphasized.

A statement of this kind certainly suggests that Protestants value their two sacraments far more highly than Catholics value their seven. It does not convey a correct idea of the Catholic doctrine regarding the sacraments, and what is described as the Protestant theory is really the old Catholic belief, which Luther did his utmost to overthrow. Our definition of a sacrament is: "A sacrament is an outward sign of inward grace, ordained by Jesus Christ, by which grace is given to our souls." Luther on the contrary declared: "It is not true that there is in the sacraments any power to justify, nor that they are signs accompanied by any grace" (*de capt. babyl.*, Wittenb., Lat. ed., II, 75). When the Pope clearly stated the Catholic doctrine on the subject of sacraments,

Luther said: "All the articles condemned by the bull are accepted by me, and I maintain that every Christian, who is to avoid everlasting damnation, must accept these articles, and all that refuse to do so, ought to be looked upon as Antichrists, and I now look upon them as pagans" (Wittenb., German ed., VII, 88). In the same dissertation against the papal bull (f. 97 b) Luther says: "There is no difference between old and new sacraments, and neither the one nor the other can convey God's grace; nothing but faith in God's signs and words gave grace in the past and still gives it now." It is true that Luther and Melanchthon, who followed him on this as on other points, subsequently expressed views approximating more closely to Catholic doctrine, and later Lutherans as a rule regarded the sacraments as channels of grace, although their Protestant prejudice did not allow them to acknowledge that they had returned to the Catholic doctrine. Consequently they are now continually obliged to discover points of difference, and first to misrepresent the teaching of the Catholic Church in order to be able to oppose her with teaching that was originally her own.

It is not true to say that seven sacraments have been recognized only since the year 1439. As early as 1140, Peter the Lombard wrote a detailed discussion of the seven sacraments which he regarded as dating from primitive times, and not a voice was raised in protest against his views. The Oriental Churches all recognized seven sacraments, and their unvarying tradition affords very strong evidence in support of them. Any one who can say that the Catholic Church has possessed seven sacraments only since the year 1439, shows his profound ignorance of Christian antiquity, unless indeed he is deliberately concealing and distorting the truth.

Even if the acts of the Council of Florence, held in 1439, contained the earliest list of the seven sacraments, it would not at all follow that they had not existed long before. Has man possessed five senses only since the year in which, for the first time, these five senses were enumerated in their usual order? No one hitherto has been able to show that any one of the seven sacraments was instituted by some Pope, bishop, or council; in the whole history of the Church we hear of no quarrels or differences of opinion such as would inevitably have occurred if any one had attempted to introduce a new sacrament, for it would have had a deep effect upon practical life. To this subject, as to others, we may apply St. Augustine's well-known words (*de bapt.*, IV, 24): "What the entire Church has always upheld, and what has not been introduced by Councils, is rightly regarded as handed down by the authority of the Apostles."

It is a strange idea that the importance of Baptism and the Lord's Supper cannot be sufficiently emphasized if we have five other sacraments in addition to them. Our Saviour was certainly not bound to institute any particular number of channels of grace, but if He chose to institute seven in order to satisfy the various needs of a soul desirous of salvation, how can any man dare to reject some of these channels and to attach peculiar importance to others? Is it, however, true that Protestants value Baptism and the Lord's Supper more highly than we do? If such were the case, we should have less reason to fear that Baptism, as administered by many Protestant ministers, is absolutely invalid. We Catholics well know the worth and sacred character of the various means of grace. Protestants need but to question any Catholic child, and they will at once be told which is the greatest and which the most indispensable sacrament, and which sacraments are intended for all men, which only for certain individuals.

To say that we ascribe to the blessings (*benedictiones*) of the Church an efficacy equal to that of the sacraments, is to repeat one of the old calumnies against things Catholic which Protestants either do not or will not understand.

Protestants are taught that by *benedictiones* we do not mean merely prayers and blessings used on particular occasions, but more especially blessings pronounced over all sorts of things ecclesiastical and domestic, such as vestments, altar cloths, candles, water, salt, edibles, oil, etc., and they believe all this to be contrary to Holy Scripture. They maintain that it is unscriptural to pray, when bread is blessed, that God will render it wholesome for body and soul, and make it a protection against all diseases and all assaults of our foes. It is unscriptural to conjure the oil, in the name of God, our Almighty Creator, that by its means all the violence of the enemy, all the hosts of the devil, all the attacks and apparitions of Satan may be expelled and overcome. It is unscriptural to ascribe to holy water power to drive out the devil and his angels, sickness and pestilence and evil passions, and to give this water to people that they may sprinkle it upon the sick, and their houses, fields, vineyards, and beds. All this is contrary to St. Paul's words, "All that is not of faith is sin" (Rom. xiv, 23). Experience proves that such practices, being of human invention, not only give rise to a false and dangerous kind of religion, but actually deter those who occupy themselves with them from attending to God's divine institutions.

"All that is not of faith is sin," and whatever is not based on the word of God is not of faith and consequently an abuse! We are inclined to ask in astonishment, Did not Christ bless bread and fishes? (Matth. xiv, 19.) Did He not give His Apostles power to heal sicknesses and to cast out devils? (Mark iii, 15), and did not they use oil (James v, 14) and the laying on of hands? (Mark xvi, 18.) Were these not outward ceremonies? What is there unscriptural in asking God to bless the things in daily use and those who employ them, since "every creature of God . . . is sanctified by the word of God and prayer" (1 Tim. iv, 4, 5)? We consider it to be quite in keeping with God's ordinance, according to which the spirit of man, whilst it dwells in his visible body, can be hindered and helped by visible things.

Thus Tobias was cured by the gall of the fish, and Naaman by washing seven times in the Jordan. In the primitive Church Christians were in the habit of sanctifying themselves and things in daily use, especially bread, water, and oil, by blessings and prayers in the name of God (e.g., Cyprian, *Ep.* 90, n. 2; Basil., *de spir. S.*, c. 27).

The blessings of the Church do not prevent Catholics from attending to things that are of divine institution, viz., the holy sacraments. Who would refrain from going to confession or Holy Communion because he uses holy water? Things blessed by the Church are intended to lead the faithful to God, the giver of all good, not to separate them from Him.

143

They ought to be used in such a way as really to convey a blessing to both body and soul.

As to the power exercised by the Church over evil spirits, we believe that it is quite scriptural (Matth. x, 1, etc.). Some kind of formula and visible sign is indispensable to the Church, but she relies chiefly upon prayer in the name of Jesus Christ, and upon confidence in His promises and His abiding and living presence in His holy Church.

Confirmation

Protestants tell us that in their opinion Confirmation, though not instituted by Christ, is nevertheless an edifying Christian rite, so it is administered in their Church with most beneficial effects. The young who are being prepared to receive the Lord's Supper for the first time, are reminded by it of their baptismal contract, they publicly profess their faith, and are solemnly admonished and pledged to be loyal towards their Creator, Redeemer, and Comforter, and then, according to Apostolic precedent, they are blessed by the laying on of hands, whilst prayer is offered on their behalf by the clergy, congregation, parents, and godparents. There is no anointing, because God's promises apply to the prayer of the congregation and not to chrism.

It seems strange that the Protestant Churches retain a ceremony not instituted by Jesus Christ. They reject as a "farce and purely human device" (Luther, Wittenb., vi, 169 b) the Sacrament of Confirmation, known and administered in the Catholic Church from the beginning, and based on Holy Scripture and tradition, and yet they retain some kind of Confirmation, of which they can give no clear account (Löhe, *Agenda*, III, 49), but which they believe to be right and fraught with blessing. In all probability, the blessing that results from preparation for Confirmation, is the opportunity for misrepresenting everything Catholic, and for impressing on the minds of the young a lifelong abhorrence of the Catholic Church. From our point of view Protestant Confirmation is a meaningless ceremony, a caricature of the Catholic rite, and incapable of conferring any graces. Confirmation is either a sacrament, an outward sign, instituted by Christ, and really communicating inward grace, or it was not instituted by our Lord, and in that case it requires no chrism or laying on of hands, nor any outward sign whatever, and effects no communication of grace. Lutherans seem to suppose that it was not regarded as a sacrament until 1439; but we find it clearly mentioned in Holy Scripture, not as the prayer of the congregation, but as a means of grace through the laying on of the Apostles' hands. Tertullian and Cyprian, writing about the year 250, as well as other doctors of the early Church, mention its administration as a true sacrament, and everywhere prevailed the belief which St. Augustine expressed in the words: "The Sacrament of Chrism is a sacrament resembling that of Baptism" (*contra lit. Petil.*, II, c. 104). Hence in Confirmation, the outward sign, viz., the anointing with chrism and the imposition of the bishop's hands, is as essential for imparting the special grace of the sacrament as is the pouring of water in Holy Baptism.

Holy Orders.

The arguments against regarding Holy Orders as a sacrament are equally unconvincing. On this subject Protestants maintain: "According to Holy Scripture, we acknowledge the office of preacher to be of divine institution, and it is the duty of preachers or pastors to make known the Gospel, to administer the sacraments, and to care for souls, and also to take part in church management, in providing for the poor, and in enforcing ecclesiastical discipline. Ministers are ordained for the discharge of these duties, that is to say, they are blessed by the laying on of hands and by prayer, and this custom dates from the Apostolic age and has always been used by the Church."

The Catholic Church on the other hand is reproached for regarding the preaching office as of no importance. A Catholic priest need never preach, but he must exercise his sacrificial and judicial functions; and according to Catholic doctrine he is a mediator between Christ and Christians. Our Lord, however, says to all: "He that cometh to me, I will not cast out; come unto me, all ye that labour and are heavy-laden; Behold, I stand at the door and knock, and if any man hear my voice and open to me the door, I will come in to him, and will sup with him and he with me."

Protestants declare that they cannot allow any one to deprive them of free access to Jesus Christ, nor to put obstacles in their way to Him.

Here we encounter again the same sort of assertion that is altogether at variance with Luther's teaching. Protestants now acknowledge that Christ appointed special officials in His Church to carry on His own work to the end of the world, and yet they refuse to recognize the position of the Catholic priesthood. Tradition, which they persist in rejecting, accepted a preaching office with which the administration of the sacraments and the care of souls are connected. Yet they are unwilling to recognize this office in the form in which it was instituted by Christ, and existed all over the Church until the time of Luther. Now Protestants want to have preachers, but no priests, such as have always existed from Apostolic times onwards in virtue of the Sacrament of Holy Orders.

It is of course true that ordination dates from the Apostolic age and has always been practised in the Church, and that the clergy are consecrated by prayer and the laying on of hands. But it is hypocritical to represent matters to the young in such a way as to lead them to believe that the priesthood, which includes the office of preacher, still exists in the Protestant Church. Whence do Protestant ministers derive their commission to teach? What guarantee has any congregation that their minister preaches the pure and unadulterated doctrine of Christ, that he has authority to govern and direct them, and that he has been admitted to the sheepfold by the right door, and is not a thief or a robber? Would Christians in the time of the Apostles have recognized a Protestant minister as their lawful teacher and shepherd? Even in the first century St. Clement of Rome spoke of the priesthood as a special state appointed by God, and distinct from the laity. St. Ignatius (ob. 107) was careful to emphasize the "cleft" between priests and laymen. St. Augustine tells us that in his time no one doubted that Holy Orders was indeed a sacrament; and at a much earlier date St. Cyprian describes the respect paid to priests. Any one who fancies that among the early Christians the clergy were preachers rather than priests, ordained to offer sacrifice and exercise judicial functions, should refer to the writings of the Fathers, and especially to those of St. Jerome and St. Chrysostom on the subject of the priesthood. He will then feel impelled to exclaim in indignation: "Ye hypocrites, who pretend to preserve the Apostolic tradition, and have really destroyed it! You have deceived the people, whom you have robbed of both altar and priests, although the latter were the guardians of Christ's teaching and the administrators of the divine mysteries. You have sent men out with no authority to teach and direct the multitude. How can you venture to assert that the Catholic priests come between Christ and His followers, and make it difficult for the weary and heavy-laden to come to our Lord? If this were true, then Christ Himself closed the door of access, by sending forth Apostles and disciples to teach in His name. The priesthood does not interfere with the mediatorial office held by Christ alone; priests are His agents, appointed to lead all the weary and sinful souls to Him, and to prepare men's hearts for the influence of divine grace so that they may 'open the door' when our Lord knocks. It is Christ Himself who teaches, baptizes, absolves, and sacrifices in the person of His priests."

But, assuming that Christ really intended the faithful to find faith, grace, and salvation without any human interposition, what have Protestant ministers to do? They do not profess to be mediators between Christ and His followers, for none may come between them. Do they not actually hinder people from having the "free access" to Christ that they profess to desire?

Again, there is no justification for the old accusation that preaching is of secondary importance in the eyes of a Catholic priest. At his ordination the bishop orders him to sacrifice, bless, and preach; and the Council of Trent declared it to be the duty of all intrusted with the care of souls, to feed the flock of which they have charge by preaching to them the word of God (sess. 23, cap. 1). Moreover the Council "commanded parish priests and those in charge of souls, to make a discourse frequently during Holy Mass, especially on Sundays and holy days" (sess. 22, cap. 8; sess. 24, cap. 4 and 7).

Samuel Laing says: "Catholicism has certainly a much stronger hold over the human mind than Protestantism. The fact is visible and undeniable, and perhaps not unaccountable." And one reason, he tells us, is because "in the Catholic Church the clergyman is more of a sacred character than it is possible to invest him with in our Protestant Church, and more cut off from all worldly affairs. The clergyman is entirely separated from individual interests, or worldly objects of ordinary life, by his celibacy. This separates him from all other men. Be their knowledge, their education, their piety, what it will, they belong to the rest of mankind in feelings, in interests, and motives of action, — he, to a peculiar class. The Catholics, who receive the elements as transubstantiated by the consecration, require very naturally and properly that the priest should be of a sanctified class, removed from human impurity, contamination, or sensual lust, as well as from all worldly affairs, as far as human nature can be. . . . Our clergy, especially in Scotland, have a very erroneous impression of the state of the Catholic clergy. . . . The education of the regular clergy of the Catholic Church is, perhaps, positively higher than the education of the Scotch clergy" (*Notes of a Traveller*, p. 394).

In virtue of his having received the Sacrament of Holy Orders, a Catholic priest is regarded by the faithful as possessing a solemn commission, and as being the minister of an infallible Church, and the messenger sent by Christ, the Son of God, whose word he makes known pure and unadulterated, just as our forefathers heard and believed it.

What benefit do Protestants derive from "the ministry of the word"? Their preachers set forth the doctrine that they have discovered by personal study of the Bible or other books. The disastrous results of this method made themselves felt even in the Reformation period, as Döllinger and Janssen have shown. Luther himself complained of his preachers that, with few exceptions, "they knew nothing of the doctrine that a knowledge of Christ and His Father alone constitutes eternal life . . . although they all succeeded in abusing the Pope, monks, and priests" (Döllinger, *Reformation*, I, 298). Does a more satisfactory state of affairs prevail at the present day? In the year 1890, Eberle, Protestant minister of Onolzheim, wrote regarding the sermons preached in the Protestant country churches in Württemberg: "I can safely assert that not a single article of faith or doctrine of Protestantism is left unchallenged, and preached consistently from every pulpit. A horrible confusion of the most conflicting opinions is preached year after year to country congregations. It is scarcely possible to imagine a more outrageous entanglement of words and beliefs. What one man preaches to-day, will be denied by another to-morrow."

What a description of Protestant worship! Sermons are necessary for the instruction and admonition of the people, and they are preached in every Catholic Church, but our worship is something more than a sermon, — it is perfect adoration of God in the Holy Sacrifice.

The Sacrament of Penance

Protestants object to many points in the Catholic doctrine regarding the Sacrament of Penance. They say that the Protestant Church also teaches the need of confession of sins to God, and under certain circumstances also to man, in addition to requiring true contrition. They distinguish repentance from confession, in which either the congregation publicly, or an individual privately, acknowledges his guilt in the presence of a minister, and is by him exhorted to have contrition and faith and to be obedient in the sight of God. This kind of confession is regarded as useful, because it tends to arouse true contrition and to soothe the consciences of those in distress of mind, but it is not a sacrament; for our Lord instituted no particular form of confession in His Church, nor did He appoint any visible sign of the invisible grace conferred.

How are we to understand the statement that under certain circumstances confession made to men is a necessary part of penance? What are these circumstances, and what is the object and effect of this confession? Either it is obligatory to confess at least grievous sins—and then it is a matter of divine commandment and not of counsel — or it is quite unnecessary. The confession of sins is made either with the intention and expectation of obtaining forgiveness — and then the minister hearing it must have authority really and truly to absolve the penitent — or with the hope of receiving merely comfort and admonition from the man to whom the penitent reveals his state and discloses his shame, — and then this confession is simply a conversation, having no particular effect on the spiritual condition of the penitent. Confession is either an essential part of a holy sacrament, ordained by Christ and based on faith, or it is a mere mockery and human device. If it is the latter, it behooves a good Protestant to say: "Away with every form of confession, away with every hope and expectation of approaching more nearly to Christ by means of this external work than by means of faith alone." If, however, confession was designed by Christ, if it leads men to Him and confers grace, then it is a true sacrament, and it itself, united with the priestly absolution, is the outward sign of the holy Sacrament of Penance with which our Lord has connected His invisible grace.

How clear and simple is the teaching of the Catholic Church on this point! She adheres to the words uttered by Christ to His disciples on the day of His resurrection: "Whose sins you shall forgive, they are forgiven them; and whose sins you shall retain, they are retained" (John xx, 23). She believes what Holy Scripture records that our Lord said on this occasion, "Receive ye the Holy Ghost." She believes that the Apostles, having received the Holy Ghost, were empowered to judge the sins of mankind in the place of God, and that their lawful successors exercise this judicial function beneficially under the guidance of the Holy Spirit. Ever since the time of the Apostles, the Church has believed not only that confession is useful in order to arouse true contrition and to soothe the consciences of those in distress of mind, but also that it is something infinitely more than this, inasmuch as it is part of this sacrament instituted by Christ to be, as a rule, the only way of obtaining forgiveness for sins committed after baptism.

Protestant Confession of Sins

The teaching of the Protestant Church seems most confused. It urges a sinner to confess his sins, and do voluntarily something that cannot fail to be unpleasant, and the minister to whom he comes is also to do something, viz., to hear and comfort him. Yet these actions are not to be regarded as visible signs of an invisible grace, although some inward efficacy is ascribed to them. To arouse contrition and soothe the conscience of one in distress of mind are undoubtedly interior acts; otherwise confession would be a mere mockery. We are told that under certain circumstances confession is a necessity, therefore it must have some effect upon the penitent's moral state, and it would seem that this effect must be a grace designed by and proceeding from Christ. Yet Protestants deny that it is anything of the kind. We have therefore in confession as practised in the Protestant Church, something external that is yet not an outward sign; something internal that is yet not an inward grace; something divine that was yet not instituted by Christ. Protestants declare this kind of confession to be far superior to that practised in the Catholic Church, because it is rare and voluntary. Ought we not to pity the multitude who have been robbed of priests invested with divine authority to forgive sins, of confession, and of the supernatural consolation imparted by sacramental absolution, and who are now invited to have recourse to this wretched substitute that is extolled as a delightful refreshment?

Can we wonder that it is a rare occurrence for any one to avail himself of this much lauded confession, whilst crowds throng around the confessionals in every Catholic Church? A sinner is not satisfied with human consolation and encouragement; the one thing that he desires in confession is to be told: "Be of good cheer, my son, thy sins are forgiven thee." He asks his confessor, as a Protestant theologian tells us (Vilmer, *Theologie der Tatsachen*, p. 90), "I want to know whether you have authority and power to forgive my sins."

In answer to the all-important questions, "Have the clergy power to forgive sins? When and by whom was this power bestowed upon each priest?" a Protestant can say nothing, but it is all perfectly simple to a Catholic.

Hear the Anglican Bishop Sparrow: "To put away all doubt, let's search the Scriptures; look into the 20th of S. John, v. 23: 'Whatsoever sins ye remit, they are remitted unto them, and whosoever sins ye retain they are retained.' Here is plainly a power of remitting sins granted to the priest by our Blessed Saviour. Nor can it be understood of remitting sins by preaching, as some expound it, nor by baptizing, as others guess, for both these, preaching and baptizing, they could do long before; but this power of remitting they receive not till now, that is, after His Resurrection" (*Sparrow's Rationale*, p. 313).

Canon Henry Liddon says in effect the same: "The power of remitting and retaining sins was given by our Risen Lord in the upper room with closed doors on the evening of the day of the Resurrection. In this way Jesus provided a remedy for the wounds which sin would leave on the souls of His redeemed" (*Secret of Clerical Power*, p. 159).

Compulsory Confession

Protestants tell us that they practise confession voluntarily, whereas in the Roman Catholic Church it is compulsory. Pope Innocent III ordered every one to confess *all* his sins at least once a year to his own parish priest; but the Council of Trent decided that the confession of only mortal sins with all their attendant circumstances, as far as a careful examination reveals them, is all that is necessary for salvation.

We read in the writings of the Fathers that all without exception, who had fallen into grievous sin after baptism, were required to confess their sins; it was a command, not a counsel. Pfaff, a Protestant historian, says: "It cannot be denied that private confession existed in the earliest ages. It would be impossible to describe it more clearly than Cyprian does" (*orig. Eccles.*, p. 134). Now St. Cyprian was so far from believing confession to be an optional thing, that he tells us how those who ventured to approach Holy Communion with impure hearts were at once punished by the avenging hand of God. That impurity of heart was due to neglect of confession appears from the fact that St. Cyprian contrasts with these sinners Christians, who frankly and with true contrition confess to God's priests even the thought of sins not actually committed (*de laps.*, c. 28). St. Augustine, Tertullian, and Origen all speak of confession as strictly necessary for sinners.

If Christ's Church really possesses authority to retain and to forgive sins, can she allow her children to avail themselves of her authority or not, just as they please? A good shepherd goes after his lost sheep, calling them and bidding them return to the sheepfold; and this is how the Church acts when she commands her children to do penance. A hireling may wait until the lost sheep comes to him of its own accord. Protestants tell us that their clergy are bound, like our own, to be silent with regard to what is said under the seal of confession. Every one intrusted with a secret is of course pledged to silence; but a Catholic priest is also called upon to administer a holy sacrament.

Enough has been said to show that it was not Innocent III who first made confession compulsory. The Fourth Lateran Council, in complete agreement with the Council of Trent, ordained that all the faithful should conform to the ancient rule laid down by our Lord Himself, and make their confession at least once a year. The only difference between the enactments of the two Councils seems to be that one requires *all* sins, the other only mortal sins to be confessed. The discrepancy is only apparent and would puzzle no one familiar with Catholic doctrines. In the time of the Fathers, as in that of Innocent III, every Catholic knew what was required then, as it is now, for a good and complete confession. If any one told him to confess all his sins, he would be quite aware that the speaker was alluding to all the sins that would debar him from salvation and involve the loss of sanctifying grace, in other words, to mortal sins. What he is bound to confess is every mortal sin, the number of times it has been committed, and not all the attendant circumstances but only such as aggravate or diminish its guilt.

The Clergy and Auricular Confession

Although Protestants speak sometimes of the beneficial results of confession, they are accustomed to ascribe various ill effects to the compulsory confession practised in the Catholic Church. They tell us: —

(1) That auricular confession is the chief means whereby the clergy control the hearts of men. Hence Jesuit missionaries proclaim: "Confession or hell; there is no middle course."

(2) That the confessional is often misused for the purpose of securing a Catholic education for the offspring of mixed marriages, contrary to a promise made previously, or in order to rouse opposition to a government disliked by the hierarchy.

(3) That many unhappy penitents have lost their innocence and been ruined, in consequence of indiscreet questions asked by a confessor. The Jesuit Gury is said to complain of this fact.

(4) That penitents are tempted to satisfy the requirements of the Church outwardly by confessing trivial sins, whilst they refrain from mentioning the more grievous sins to which they are in bondage; or they fancy themselves free, after confession and absolution, to sin again, knowing that they can easily be absolved. It cannot therefore be denied that compulsory confession as practised in the Roman Catholic Church is fraught with danger to souls. This is acknowledged by a conscientious Catholic priest to be the case.

(1) It is a truth founded upon divine revelation, that as a rule confession is the only means of saving a grievous sinner from hell. The Jesuits did not invent this theory, nor is it taught exclusively by them. Neither Jesuits nor any other priests hear confessions with the intention of thus obtaining influence over their penitents, but in order to preserve souls from hell. Auricular confession was not instituted to gratify any desire for power on the part of the clergy, and if any one really believes that it owes its origin to such a desire, what is, in his opinion, the object with which a Protestant minister hears a private confession, and gives advice and encouragement to erring and doubting hearts?

(2) In the confessional a Catholic is frequently reminded of his duties, but no one can regard this as a misuse of con-

fession any more than we Catholics have a right to complain if a Protestant minister tries to prevent a mixed marriage. It is very strange that any one can suppose it to be the duty of a Catholic priest to say nothing at all, or even to express approval, if the children of Catholic parents are brought up outside the Church.

It is absolutely false to assert that the confessional is used for stirring up resistance to authority. This is not the place whence rebels and rioters derive their turbulent ideas.

(3) Father Gury, a Jesuit, was the author of a book for the guidance of confessors in the exercise of their difficult office. We owe him a debt of gratitude for warning priests against asking indiscreet questions and for pointing out the harm that such questions may cause. But it is foolish and unreasonable to condemn the confessional, which is a school of virtue and a source of grace, because individual confessors have been imprudent. It would be equally absurd to try to deter the sick from consulting a physician, because instances have occurred of patients suffering injury at the hands of an unskilful doctor.

(4) It is a universally recognized fact that the best and most beneficial institutions are liable to misuse. Thus a frivolous Catholic may perhaps abuse the privilege of confession, but the sacrament could be answerable for this abuse only if it sanctioned it. This is, however, by no means the case; every Catholic child is taught that if forgiveness is to be obtained, it is not enough to confess one's sins, but the confession must be accompanied by true, supernatural contrition arising out of love of God, and also by an earnest purpose of amendment, otherwise no sin can be forgiven. It is a fearful sacrilege to refrain from motives of false shame, or because one does not intend to renounce them, from all allusion to the grievous sins to which one is in bondage.

Priests are bound to encourage their people to make a good use of the Sacrament of Penance, and in this way they will lead the faulty nearer to that perfection at which we all aim in this world but to which we cannot yet attain. Are all Protestants so perfect that none ever fall back into some sinful habit, even after making a public or private confession and receiving the Lord's Supper? Do none of them return year after year to their pastor to hear once more the tidings of forgiveness? Does such a Protestant derive greater help towards final perseverance than a Catholic in the tribunal of penance? It is unfair and dishonourable to find fault with the Catholic confessional and not to mention the unspeakable good that it achieves; although many impartial non-Catholics bear testimony to the great benefits resulting from it. It is enough to name Voltaire, the father of modern unbelief, and Rousseau, and men like Goethe, Wilhelm von Humboldt, Leibnitz, and Pestalozzi. Zezschwitz, a Protestant professor of theology, says: "We Protestants ought to leave off judging unfairly, and looking at only one side of a question. . . . No one can ever have glanced at the better sort of Catholic books on morals, who fancies that all the debated points between ourselves and Catholics can be settled simply by reviving the old charges regarding the unscrupulous and disastrous use of the confessional. There are faults on both sides. I need only allude to confessors such as Carlo Borromeo and Philip Neri, the latter a penitent of the Jesuits, and himself one of the most charming, liberal-minded, and sympathetic confessors who ever lived."

"There is another circumstance connected with the institutions of that Church," says François Guizot, the great French historian, "which has not, in general, been so much noticed as it deserves. I allude to its penitentiary system, which is the more interesting in the present day, because, so far as the principles and applications of moral law are concerned, it is almost completely in unison with the notions of modern philosophy. . . . It is sufficiently evident that repentance and example were the objects proposed by the Church in every part of its system of penance. And is not the attainment of these very objects the end of every truly philosophical legislation? Is it not for the sake of these very principles that the most enlightened lawyers have clamoured for Europe?" (*History of Civilization.*)

Satisfaction for Sins

Finally Protestants declare that all idea of satisfaction is altogether foreign to them, as Christ by His perfect obedience to God's will and especially by His Passion and Death, made abundant satisfaction for our sins. Catholic priests nevertheless impose penances intended partly to satisfy God's justice for sins committed, and partly to act as a safeguard against future falls into sin. These penances consist chiefly in almsgiving, fasting, and repeating certain prayers. How little importance is attached to the spiritual state of the person who performs these works is apparent from the fact that one can make satisfaction for another, and this is frequently done in return for payment of money.

It is quite true that all idea of satisfaction is foreign to Protestantism, which looks only at the infinite satisfaction made by Christ whereby He merited all grace and the remission of all our sins and penalties. The Catholic Church is by no means blind to our Lord's atonement and thankfully acknowledges it, but she goes further, and instead of stopping short at the thought "Christ suffered for us," she asks: "Have I personally nothing more to do in order to make the merits of Christ my own? If I personally have sinned and offended God, and hope to be forgiven because Christ has made satisfaction for me, is that all which is required of me, or ought I to do anything myself in reparation for the wrong committed against God?" The answer to this question is perfectly clear: "If we suffer in expiation of our sins, we become like Jesus Christ who made atonement for us and from whom all our powers are derived. We rely, moreover, on the promise that if we suffer with Him we shall be glorified with Him. No satisfaction that we can offer for our sins is ours in the sense of being independent of Jesus Christ. We can indeed do nothing of ourselves, but we can do all things in Him who strengtheneth us. Man has in himself nothing whereof to glory, but all our glory is in Christ in whom we live, merit, and make satisfaction, if we bring forth worthy

157

fruits of penance, fruits that derive all their efficacy from Him, that are by Him offered up to the Father and that are accepted by the Father for His sake" (Trident, sess., 14. 8 cap.).

Holy Scripture contains many instances of punishment in- flicted by God upon men whose sins were forgiven, and many also of satisfaction and penance by means of which a sinner sought to win the grace of God and to avert His punishments. The Prodigal Son asked to become one of his father's hired servants; the thought would never have occurred to him, had he not reasoned thus: "I owe some reparation to my father, although in his love he is willing to forgive me all the wrong that I have done him." The following remarkable passage was written by Luther (assert. 41, *art. contra indulg. ad art.* 5): "Our mother, the Christian Church, wishing to anticipate the punishments inflicted by the hand of God, chas- tizes her children with some sort of reparation that they may not fall under His rod. Thus did the Ninivites, by their self-imposed labours, anticipate the judgment of God. This voluntary punishment is necessary, for sins are punished either by us, or by men, or by God, although others [i.e., Catholics] get rid of them altogether by means of indul- gences. If they were good shepherds they would rather im- pose penalties, and follow the example of the churches in anticipating God's judgment."

Hence at this period, Luther thought that heavier penal- ties ought to be inflicted; he did not propose to abolish them and leave everything to Christ. Subsequently, however, he condemned all idea of satisfaction made by men, although even then he confessed that his views were contrary to those of the early Christians and of the majority of mankind. In his opinion, this erroneous theory of satisfaction had existed from the beginning of the world; many great men had done their best to overthrow it, but it would probably remain until the end of all things (*Op.* Jen., V, 816).

Protestants believe that Catholics undertake for payment to make reparation for the sins of others, and this alleged practice is regarded as evidence of the slight importance attached to the disposition of the sinner when a penance is imposed. The Council of Trent and all the doctors of the Church make it obligatory upon the confessor to adapt the penance that he imposes both to the magnitude of the offence and the disposition of the penitent. It would be quite impossible to discover, anywhere in the world, a Catholic who had received payment for performing another's penance, or who had attempted to bribe another to perform the penance imposed upon him. Yet our antagonists do not hesitate to explain publicly how it is all arranged. They refer to a chapter in the Roman Catechism (II, 5, 72) which, however, does not apply to penances imposed on individuals for definite, personal sins. Alexander VII actually condemned the proposition (prop. 15) that one sinner might appoint some one to perform his penance in his stead. Least of all is there any allusion to payment of money. The Roman Catechism simply proclaims the profound truth, firmly based on Holy Scripture and on the life of the early Church, that by means of voluntary works of penance, or willingly endured suffering, one Christian can help another. Unless this were true no one could intercede for sinners, but it follows necessarily from the Communion of Saints. In proof of it, reference may be made to Abraham's prayer for the people of Sodom, to St. Paul's exhortation to his converts that they should "bear one another's burdens" (Gal. vi, 2), and to a panegyric quoted by Eusebius (V, 2) and uttered by the clergy of Lyons over the martyrs of that city: "They were not filled with arrogance towards the fallen, but with motherly compassion they shared with others that wherein they abounded, and shed many tears for them before God." Eusebius records elsewhere (III, 24) that St. John the Apostle exclaimed to a young man who had committed a robbery: "I will make satisfaction for thee; thou hast still hope of safety; for thy sake I will gladly welcome death, even as our Lord died for us." Moses offered to be a scapegoat for the people of Israel (Exod. xxxii, 32), and St. Paul even went so far as to wish to be anathema from Christ for the sake of his brethren (Rom. ix, 3). Any one who reflects over these passages will find no difficulty in understanding the sentence in the Roman Catechism.

Matrimony

Protestants tell us that they regard matrimony as an ordinance instituted by God, but not as a sacrament, because it can be contracted outside the Church. Christ did not alter or add to this ordinance, but reinforced it and promised special blessings to married Christians. Hence this state is called that of "Holy Matrimony," and according to the procedure of the early Church it ought to be entered upon before Christian witnesses and with prayer and exhortation from the word of God.

The Catholic Church calls matrimony a sacrament, but forbids it to her priests, thus showing that she looks upon it as an inferior state. In the Bible we read that a bishop should be the husband of one wife, and that it is a devilish doctrine to forbid men to marry. The Christian Church adhered to scriptural teaching on this subject for a thousand years, and it was not until the eleventh century that compulsory celibacy was introduced by Pope Gregory VII.

Statements of this sort require careful consideration. Let us ask, in the first instance, what the Catholic Church thinks of marriage, and what Luther's views were on the subject. Which doctrine harmonizes best with Holy Scripture and with the opinions of Christian antiquity? The Catholic belief with regard to marriage is this: God Himself instituted it in Paradise as an indissoluble bond uniting one man and one woman. Jesus undoubtedly altered and added to this ordinance and through His Apostles promised peculiar blessings to married people, for He raised marriage to the dignity of a real sacrament. That our Lord intended to make it something more than it had become among both Jews and pagans is plain from His words in Matth. xix, 3, etc., Mark x, 2, etc., Luke xvi, 18, and especially from St. Paul's instructions in 1 Cor. vii and Ephes. v. The Apostle regarded even the vocation to the married life as a special grace of God (1 Cor. vii, 7); he did not consider the marriage of unbelievers as on a level with Christian marriage (v. 13), but taught that an unbelieving husband could be sanctified by his Christian wife and vice versa (v. 14). He compares the marriage bond with the union existing between Christ and the Church (Ephes. v, 29), this union being her actual source of grace, and he calls this union a great sacrament (or mystery) adding, "I speak in Christ and in the Church" (v. 32). How could St. Paul say that marriage resembles Christ's union with the Church unless grace was communicated by means of it? If Protestants examined more carefully the view taken of matrimony in the early Church, they would find that it was always regarded as a sacrament. This can be easily proved from the writings of Tertullian, St. Ambrose, and St. Augustine (cf. Schanz, *Sakramentenlehre*, pp. 726–738).

The Catholic Church undoubtedly considers the married state holy. Did Luther value it equally or even more highly? Let us quote his own words on the subject: "Marriage does not concern the Church at all, but is outside her sphere, being a temporal and worldly thing" (Walch, XXII, 1748; XII, 1721; VII, 668). "Know that marriage is an external, bodily thing, like any other worldly business" (Jen. ed., II, 153).

Of the enduring character of this sacrament in the Catholic Church, Goethe notes in his *Autobiography* that "Here a youthful pair give their hands to one another, not for a passing salutation, or for the dance; the priest pronounces his blessing upon the act, and the bond is indissoluble."

A youthful pair? What does Lecky say in this regard? "The nearly universal custom of early marriages among the Irish peasantry has alone rendered possible that high standard of female chastity, that intense and zealous sensitiveness respecting female honour, for which . . . the Irish poor have long been prominent in Europe" (*European Morals*, II., 153).

The Catholic Church has always insisted upon the unity of the marriage bond, adhering thus to Christ's teaching that

God instituted marriage in order to unite one man and one woman (Matth. xix, 3, etc.), and that in His kingdom this unity must be restored and maintained. Luther, on the contrary, allowed Count Philip of Hesse to take a second wife during the lifetime of his lawful spouse. The preacher who performed the ceremony had three wives, all living, and in his discourse he tried to soothe the bride's conscientious scruples by telling her that bigamy had hitherto been forbidden among Christians in consequence of their misunderstanding Holy Scripture. Luther himself declared several times in his sermons that a man was not forbidden to have more than one wife; he did not himself recommend polygamy but could not prohibit it (Janssen, *An meine Kritiker*, II, 91).

Indissolubility of Marriage

The Catholic Church insists upon the indissolubility no less than upon the unity of marriage. She has always respected our Lord's words: "What God hath joined together, let no man put asunder" (Matth. xix, 6); "Whosoever shall put away his wife, except it be for fornication, and shall marry another, committeth adultery; and he that shall marry her that is put away, committeth adultery" (v. 9). These words sanction separation from an adulteress, but not the remarriage of either party. The disciples clearly understood them in this sense, for they exclaimed: "If the case of a man with his wife be so, it is not expedient to marry" (v. 10). In Mark x, 2–12 and Luke xvi, 18 our Lord absolutely forbids any severance of the marriage bond. Should any doubt still linger in the mind of one who has studied these passages, it cannot fail to be removed by reference to 1 Cor. vii, 10, 11, where St. Paul writes: "To them that are married, not I, but the Lord commandeth that the wife depart not from her husband. And if she depart, that she remain unmarried. . . . And let not the husband put away his wife." The Catholic Church has invariably upheld this doctrine. It is notorious that Henry VIII, King of England, requested Pope Clement VII to divorce him from his lawful wife. The

Pope went as far as he possibly could go in order to concili-
ate the king, enduring all sorts of abuse and reproaches,
but he could not surrender the sanctity of marriage, and
defied Henry rather than disobey God. To his intense sorrow the Holy Father saw the king and his kingdom fall
away from the faith, but he could not, on that account, permit what the Gospel forbade. How different was Luther's
line of action towards Philip of Hesse! He taught and publicly preached opinions utterly at variance with the Biblical
and early Christian views on marriage. Not only did he
sanction the divorce on his own authority, and in opposition
to Holy Scripture, but from the pulpit he defended principles regarding married life, such as had never been heard
before in any Christian country, and he even declared adultery to be permissible. Evers, a Protestant pastor who was
subsequently reconciled to the Catholic Church, says of
Luther: "Is it possible that a man, capable of propounding
such shamelessness to the people, in his public sermons and
writings, can have been the instrument, chosen by God, for
the reformation of the Church?" (*Katholisch oder Protes-
tantisch*, p. 408).

The Rev. A. K. Blois, of the First Baptist Church, Chicago,
said: "The attitude of the Roman Catholic Church is admirable. It is better to be too strict than too loose in all
questions of morals, and especially in this [divorce] question,
which so vitally affects both public and private welfare."

Rev. Dr. Morgan Dix, Episcopalian, rejoices that "Roman
Catholics — all honor to them! — allow no divorce *a vinculo*,
following literally the command of our Lord Jesus Christ"
(*Lectures on the Calling of a Christian Woman*).

At one moment we are told that the Catholic Church sets
too high a value upon matrimony by regarding it as a sacrament, at another we hear that she degrades it by forbidding
her priests to marry. This is another of those contradictions to which Protestants are prone. The Catholic doctrine
on the subject is very simple: In the Church of Christ matrimony is raised above the purely natural order, and becomes

a means of grace. It does not, however, follow that the married state is the highest in the kingdom of Christ. On the contrary, it is surpassed by voluntary virginity, preserved through love of God, according to the teaching and example of our Lord Himself and His Apostles. What for every Christian is a matter of counsel (cf. Matth. xix, 12 and 1 Cor. vii, 7, 8), is imposed by the Church as a binding obligation upon her priests, since their office requires of them a higher degree of perfection.

The Catholic Church does not forbid marriage, and follows St. Paul (1 Tim. iv, 1) in calling such prohibition "a doctrine of devils." No one ought to write a treatise on religion without knowing to what subjects these devilish doctrines refer. According to them, all marriage is forbidden, and the Catholic Church teaches nothing of the kind. But, on the other hand, she does not command any one to marry, and in this respect she differs from Luther, who declared perpetual chastity to be impossible and continence to be a crime. Schön, a Protestant, in writing of Luther, says: "He was probably the first, since the foundation of the Christian Church, to teach that man was a slave to his sexual impulses, and that the commandment to marry was not only binding upon every one, but of far stricter obligation than the commandments in the Decalogue which forbid murder and adultery."

Moreover, it behooves every theologian to understand what St. Paul meant by saying that a bishop should be the husband of one wife (1 Tim. iii, 2). If he meant that a bishop ought to be a married man, why did he not himself take a wife instead of wishing that all were as he was? If it is a diabolical doctrine to require those who wish to serve Christ perfectly and feel called to this service to remain unmarried, how could St. Paul extol virginity as the higher way? It is absolute hypocrisy to try to destroy the old Christian doctrines, to strip marriage of its supernatural character and make it a purely natural business, like agriculture or carpentry, and at the same time to blame the Catholic Church for teaching the doctrines of devils, whereas within her fold alone marriage is still regarded as a holy state on which peculiar blessings are bestowed, and as a means for attaining to the supernatural end of man. We have no fear that the Apostles will ever judge us for possessing diabolical doctrines; they will rather discover such things elsewhere; for there are some theories regarding marriage which St. Paul would certainly not acknowledge to have been taught by Christ and himself.

Compulsory Celibacy

Protestants are taught that in the eleventh century Gregory VII introduced compulsory celibacy, although for over a thousand years the Church had followed St. Paul and condemned it as a doctrine of devils. It ought not to be necessary at the present day to refute this statement, but it recurs with obstinate persistency. When the disciples exclaimed, "It is not expedient to marry," our Lord did not explain that, on the contrary, they all ought to take to themselves wives, but remarked that some were voluntarily continent for the sake of the kingdom of heaven. This is recorded in Holy Scripture, as also is St. Paul's recommendation of celibacy. It is certain, too, that from the beginning many Christians have led chaste and virginal lives in order to serve God better. Was it not quite natural for the Church to require her priests to lead the life which all Christians regarded as peculiarly pure and perfect, and which many adopted of their own free will? Pilatus, a Protestant whose works have done much to overthrow many Protestant prejudices, says (*Quos ego*, 17 and 18): "Celibacy was not introduced by the Pope, but was due to the priests' desire for the union with God resulting from conquest of the passions." In the primitive Church, where baptism was administered generally only to adults, it was impossible to ordain none but unmarried men to the priesthood. If such restrictions had existed, where could St. Paul and St. Timothy have found men fit to be priests and bishops? But even in the Apostolic age St. Paul insisted that no one who had been married more than once should be consecrated bishop. We never hear of any priest marrying after his ordination, although many rules were made on the subject such as those of the Council of Neocaesarea in 314 (can. 1), according to which a priest was to be degraded if he took a wife. The Second Council of Carthage in 390 declared the celibacy of the clergy to have been ordered by the Apostles themselves. In the tenth century the old law of the Church was frequently disregarded, and consequently Gregory VII, like several of his predecessors, drew attention to it and insisted upon its observance. In this way he prevented any further decay of ecclesiastical discipline and order, and we owe him a debt of gratitude for what he did, but celibacy was not introduced by him. It would be possible to charge the Catholic Church with violence and compulsion only if she forced men into the priesthood, and then constrained them to lead a celibate existence. Priests are not, like recruits for the army in some countries, obtained by means of conscription. Before a bishop confers the subdiaconate, he says: "You are still free to adopt a secular calling if you desire, but when you have received this order, you will no longer be able to draw back, but you will serve God, and with His help observe chastity. Therefore reflect, whilst there is yet time." Every Catholic priest can say: "Was I not at liberty to use my freedom? To whom was I bound, when I voluntarily remained unmarried?" He avails himself of true Apostolic freedom, when of his own accord for Christ's sake and in order to save his soul, he renounces rights possessed hitherto. Luther professed to combat celibacy because of his regard for morality, but we can form some idea of his real opinions from a passage in a letter, where he says (*Werke*, 29, 17, etc.): "Even if one or two, or a hundred or a thousand councils decided that the clergy might marry, he, Luther, would rather put up with one who had been unchaste all his life, than with one who took a wife after such a decision had been made. He wished to command as God's representative and to give advice, so that no one on the strength of such a decision should take a wife and endanger his salvation, but rather let every one live in chastity, and if that is impossible, let him not despond in his sin and frailty, but appeal to God's mercy." Is this the language of a serious man, concerned about truth and justice, or is it not rather that of a child determined to do what his mother has forbidden?

"The chaste influence of the celibate clergy of Ireland," says the anti-Irish Froude, "kept the peasants wonderfully moral. Wealthy men may sleep in Ireland with unlocked doors with a security that no police in New York or London could secure, so absolutely honest are the people. Offenses of impurity, also, are almost entirely unknown" (*New York Times*, Oct. 25, 1872).

Extreme Unction

Protestants dispense altogether with Extreme Unction, and ask where in the Bible we discover that Satan is to be driven out of the oil, and that the dying are to be anointed with oil thus exorcised? Where are we promised that anointing of this kind leads to the forgiveness of sins committed through the sense of sight, etc. The passage in James v, 14 refers to the sick and their recovery, not to the dying. Anointing with oil is a very ancient remedy, but the chief importance is attached to the prayer of faith. In primitive times the dying relied only on the consolation supplied by Holy Communion, which was called the "Viaticum" and the "medicine of immortality"; and in the Protestant Church it still continues to be their last comfort.

We have here an ingenious attempt to lay stress upon side issues and disregard the chief point. Allusion is made to Holy Communion, but the real question is: Did Christ intend the dying to receive, besides Holy Communion, another means of grace to console and cure them in their hour of need? The Bible and tradition both answer this question in the affirmative. Leibnitz, a Protestant, says: "No lengthy discussion of Extreme Unction is required. The custom of administering it finds support both in Holy Scripture and in the Church's interpretation of the same, on which Catholics rely with assurance." How and when did Extreme Unction come to be regarded as a sacrament, if it was not always recognized as such in the Church? No one can offer any explanation.

Protestants ask contemptuously where, in Holy Scripture, we discover that Satan is to be driven out of the oil, and that the dying are to be anointed with oil thus exorcised. The Catholic Church knows that there are in the Bible several references to the curse under which the whole world was laid on account of the sins of mankind, and St. Paul says that every creature groaneth for deliverance from it (Rom. viii, 21, 22). Moreover, we read much about Satan and his influence, and find that Christ, who triumphed over Satan, gave His Apostles power over evil spirits (Matth. x, 1). Therefore, when the Church requires the water used in Baptism and the oil employed in Extreme Unction to be previously blessed, and when she includes exorcisms in the prayers read on these occasions, she is doing nothing contrary to the word of God. The Sacrament of Extreme Unction, however, exists independently of the forms prescribed by the Church for blessing the oil used in its administration.

Another question asked by Protestants is: "Where are we promised that anointing of this kind leads to the forgiveness of sins committed through the sense of sight, etc.?" Surely those who ask this question cannot read, for the answer stands clearly in St. James' epistle: "If he [the sick man] be in sins, they shall be forgiven him." Does not this satisfy them? The statement that the passage in St. James v refers not to the dying, but to the sick and their recovery, is unintelligible, for are not the dying sick? Or do we administer Extreme Unction only to those of whose restoration to health no hope remains? Does not every catechism contain a warning not to delay too long the administration of this sacrament, since it is intended to benefit the sick in body as well as in soul? Protestants are taught that anointing with oil is a very ancient remedy, and that the chief importance is attached to the prayer of faith. It is, of course, quite true that oil is a very ancient and usual remedy, just as water is the usual means of cleansing, and bread the usual form of nourishment. Oil, water, and bread serve these purposes in the realm of nature, but when, in conformity with divinely given instructions, the prayer of faith is added to them, they become outward signs of supernatural grace in the holy sacraments. Neither water, nor bread, nor oil alone, nor even the prayer of faith alone, effects what our Lord intended the sacraments to do. The word of God undeniably contains plain allusions to oil, to the prayer of faith, and to forgiveness of sins, as well as to restoration to health.

Finally, Protestants maintain that in the primitive Church the sick relied solely upon the consolation derived from Holy Communion. Apart from the fact that the sick in those days received the real sacrament of Holy Communion and not the Protestant Last Supper, there is abundant testimony in very ancient writings proving that Extreme Unction was always regarded as a sacrament, and that no innovations were made in its administration. Allusions to it occur in the works of St. Irenaeus (died 207) and of Origen (died 254).

Baptism

Protestants maintain with regard to Holy Baptism that the only difference between themselves and Catholics is that the latter believe original sin to be completely removed by this sacrament, whereas Protestants think that our natural sinfulness remains.

This difference has already been discussed, and it is unnecessary to say more here than that we are very thankful that Luther retained the old Catholic doctrine on the subject of Baptism, and carried with him into Protestantism a remnant of genuine Catholicism, which seems there rather out of place. Luther thought, however, that any one who chose might refuse to be baptized. The fact that true Baptism remains in the Protestant Churches is the cause of salvation to countless souls, especially to those of children. Unhappily the sacrament is not always validly administered, for Protestants do not always baptize in the name of the Blessed

Trinity, nor are they careful that the water should flow. There are some ministers who openly acknowledge that they wish to see Baptism abolished.

The Holy Eucharist

On the subject of the Holy Eucharist, Protestants refer to transubstantiation, the Sacrifice of the Mass, and the withdrawal of the chalice from the laity, as the three points of Catholic doctrine to which they take exception.

The Protestant doctrine is, we are told, that in the Holy Eucharist they really receive the Body and Blood of Christ together with the blessed bread and wine, but the sacramental species continue really to be bread and wine and do not merely appear to be such. In this belief they follow the teaching of St. Paul (1 Cor. x, 16). They think therefore that in the Bible two elements, one earthly and one heavenly, are distinguished, although they are united in a most intimate and incomprehensible manner.

The average Protestant has no idea how difficult it was for Luther to discover any foundation for this theory. He accepts what he is taught and believes that in the Holy Eucharist he receives bread and wine as well as the Body and Blood of Christ, whilst Catholics adhere to an unscriptural doctrine, and believe that Christ alone is present under the species of bread and wine.

Luther would have liked to give the words used by our Lord at the Last Supper a figurative interpretation, but they seemed too clear and forcible for this to be possible. Therefore he interpreted them literally, but abandoned all idea of transubstantiation. How he reconciled the absence of transubstantiation with the Real Presence of Christ is quite incomprehensible, nor can any one follow Luther's own arguments. Hence, as a rule, all living faith in the Real Presence has disappeared, giving place to a theory which would not have seemed hard even to the Jews in the synagogue at Capharnaum.

Transubstantiation, as taught by the Catholic Church, is a deep mystery, but in believing it we do at least know what we believe and why we believe it. We know that we are not accepting the view of a professor who has imagined something that none of the early Christians ever heard of, but we are holding fast to the tradition of centuries based on our Lord's own words. If the Catholic doctrine regarding the Holy Eucharist were erroneous, we should surely know with whom and when it originated, as before that time men must have believed something else. But this is certainly not the case; the same doctrine can be traced back to the Cenaculum in Jerusalem and to the Last Supper, when our Lord uttered the words, "This is my Body."

By his word a king can change a death warrant into a reprieve, so that instead of being the harbinger of sorrow and death it becomes the bearer of joy and life, yet the paper on which he writes is unchanged. A dog cannot distinguish any difference in the document, as it was when presented to the monarch and as it is after passing through his hands; but a human being perceives an infinite change effected by the king's words. In the same way, by the supernatural light of faith, we recognize the transubstantiation, which is imperceptible to our natural reason, relying as it does upon our senses. We believe that through the action of Christ's words, the outward form belonging to the substance of ordinary bread now clothes the living Bread, which came down from heaven in order that all who eat thereof may live forever. In other words the substance of the bread is changed into the Body of our Lord Jesus Christ, but the outward qualities or species of bread remain unaffected, just as the paper remains the same, whether it conveys a death warrant or a pardon.

St. Paul says nothing contrary to the unvarying belief in transubstantiation. He speaks, it is true, of the Holy Eucharist as *bread*, but his meaning, which is more important than the actual word, is clear (1 Cor. x, 16, 17; xi, 26, 28). There can be no doubt as to the doctrine of the Catholic Church, and yet she too calls the consecrated host "bread of heaven," "angels' bread." Moreover, the Greek word used by St. Paul signifies food rather than bread. Before the time of Luther, no one understood St. Paul to mean what Luther supposed. On the contrary, he has always been quoted in support of the Catholic doctrine, since he asserts that the chalice of benediction, which we bless, is the communion of the Blood of Christ, and the bread, which we break, is the partaking of the Body of the Lord.

It is here impossible to do more than refer to one or two of the countless witnesses to this belief. St. Justin (died 166) says: "We are taught that'this consecrated food is the flesh and blood of the Son of God. Since Christ Himself said of the bread, This is my Body, who can doubt the fact? and since He said, This is my Blood, who would venture to suppose that it is not His Blood? He changed water into wine; why should we not believe that He changes wine into blood?" Such was the doctrine taught in the fourth century by St. Cyril to his catechumens in Jerusalem. All the regulations for public worship in the early Church refer to transubstantiation, and the Russian Church retains this doctrine as an article of faith.

Transubstantiation

We are told by Protestants, moreover, that the Catholic doctrine regarding transubstantiation contains an unscriptural statement to the effect that in the mass priests by means of their miraculous power create God, the Creator of all things (Böhmer, *Jus Eccles. protest.*, V, 192).

Divinely revealed truth contains profound mysteries which, when stated in human language, are apt to be distorted and exaggerated or even ridiculed. Hence the early Christians, in obedience to our Lord's exhortation not to throw pearls before swine, were careful to keep their sacred mysteries secret from the heathen. But any one who undertakes to teach young Protestants the doctrinal points distinguishing Catholicism and Protestantism ought first to ascertain what our doctrines really are. When any one hears that in the mass priests profess to create the Creator, he naturally supposes that Catholic priests set themselves above God who created them. But this is a complete misrepresentation.

The priest does not create the Creator, but the word of Christ changes the bread and wine into His Body and Blood. The priest may be the agent of this mysterious transaction, but he is acting simply as Christ's servant and in accordance with His instructions. It is Christ who baptizes, Christ who preaches, Christ who absolves, and Christ who effects transubstantiation, — not the priest. It is not the men designing and printing bank notes who change the worthless paper into money; it is the will of those who employ these workmen. In the same way God's word does everything and a priest nothing unless he be divinely commissioned.

Perhaps we may be permitted to ask who creates the Creator in the Protestant rite. Protestants are taught that Christ is really received in Holy Communion, but how does He become present? Does He come when the minister blesses the bread and wine, and utters over them the words of institution? In that case the minister possesses greater powers than other men enjoy and must be a real priest, which he does not claim to be. Or does the recipient of the bread and wine do anything which causes him to receive Christ together with them? In that case, what would be the good of any minister, or of any rite, and where in the Bible can we find such power promised to every individual, for if this were true each man would be able to bless and consecrate?

Protestants allege further that our doctrines regarding the consecrated host are unscriptural, for we teach that divine honour should be paid it, and that Christ with His sacred Body, divinity, and humanity, can be kept in the monstrance and carried in procession on Corpus Christi and other festivals. Corpus Christi was instituted by Urban IV in 1264, and the Council of Trent ordered it to be observed in order to wound, humiliate, or convert heretics and to celebrate the triumph of Catholicism over them. It is notorious that ever since the memorable celebration of the feast at Augsburg in 1530, Protestants have on this day been exposed to much ill treatment and many insults, in consequence of which they were warned not to take part in the festival from motives of curiosity.

It seems impossible to believe that Christ is really received in Holy Communion and at the same time to refuse Him adoration. Luther says that whoever believes in the Real Presence of Christ cannot without sin refuse to reverence the sacrament, but that those who do not adore it, are not to be branded as heretics. In fact, he says, it is better not to adore it (Wittenb., VII, 343 ff.). The oldest Christian liturgy, that of St. James, requires the deacon to exclaim: "Let us adore and extol the living Lamb of God, offered upon the altar!" Adoration follows as a matter of course from belief in the Real Presence of Christ, and, according to Catholic belief, this adoration is given to Christ, the Son of God, present under the form of bread.

The Catholic Church has always understood the words "This is my Body" to mean that what appears to be bread is not really bread but the Body of Christ (St. Cyril of Jerusalem), and if this is the case before the sacred hosts are consumed, Christ must remain also in those which have not been consumed as long as the outward form remains unchanged. Therefore He can be kept in the tabernacle to be taken as Viaticum to the dying, and exposed in the monstrance to the veneration of the faithful. The feast of Corpus Christi is the exultant expression of our joy and gratitude for the inestimable favour bestowed upon us by our Saviour in remaining permanently in the midst of His people. The feast was established long before there were any Protestants to be offended at it, and Catholics, when they celebrate it, have no idea of triumphing over others, nor of wounding, humiliating, and converting them. That Corpus Christi processions are occasions when Protestants are ill treated and insulted is one of those fictions to which non-Catholics adhere with most unreasonable tenacity, and we have never heard of their being exposed to outrages on this festival. No harm happened to them at Augsburg in 1530, but the Protestant princes by their words and actions insulted the emperor, who was himself carrying a lighted taper behind the Blessed Sacrament.

We have no objection at all to the rule that Protestants are not to take part in our processions from motives of curiosity, but we should like to suggest that, if by any chance they see or meet such a procession, they should conform to the ordinary rules of politeness and decency.

The Sacrifice of the Mass

Protestants do their utmost to misrepresent and abuse the Holy Sacrifice of the Mass, in order to inspire the young, who are incapable of examining facts for themselves, with hatred and abhorrence of Catholicism. They say that originally the Mass was nothing but the usual public celebration of Holy Communion, in which the fruits of Christ's atoning death were perpetually applied to the Christians present. This is still the Protestant doctrine, only instead of "Mass," they speak of the Lord's Supper. Roman Catholicism, however, has made additions to this simple celebration of Holy Communion, and has thus changed it into a sacrifice of atonement, offered by the priests, although this is contrary to God's command and promises.

It would be only fair to consider first the reason given by Luther for abolishing the Mass. He tells us that one night the devil appeared to him, and in fearful tones, curdling his very blood, declared that he, the learned Dr. Luther, had practised idolatry every day for fifteen years by saying Mass. Although Luther was quite aware that the devil was not speaking the truth, he abolished the Mass and priestly ordination (Wittenb., Germ. ed., VII, 443; Jena, VI, 87; Walch, XIX, 1489). In spite of knowing his doctrines to be opposed to his own innermost convictions and to the unanimous belief of antiquity, he demanded unconditional acceptance of them, and expressed himself in language such as no Pope or Doctor of the Church had ever used. He said: "No one, since the world has existed, ever taught as I, Dr. Martin Luther, teach. I care nothing for all the texts of Scripture. I need no foundation for my doctrines, my will takes the place of all arguments. I, Dr. Martin Luther, will have it thus. I am wiser than all the rest of the world put together" (Wittenb., V, 107).

We see, therefore, who abolished the Holy Sacrifice of the Mass, and to whom Luther ascribed his impulse to take this step. But who instituted the sacrifice? It existed from the very beginning, and no one doubted that it was of divine origin. No bold innovator ever came forward proclaiming, "The priest at the altar offers a true sacrifice of reconciliation," nor was there any one who ventured to foist the idea of sacrifice upon the Church founded by Christ, in opposition to the will of her divine Founder. The bishops have always expressed the feeling of the Church, and would promptly have resisted so important an innovation as the Mass, if it had really been superimposed upon the old Communion service; but there is no trace of any such thing in the whole history of the Church, and honest Protestants now acknowledge this to be the truth. Kahnis, for instance, writes (*Die Kirche*, 1865, p. 113), "The Eucharist is a sacrifice"; and Thiersch says, "As our knowledge of ancient Christianity has increased, it has become clearer to Protestant theologians, that in the very earliest ritual and in all ancient liturgies the Eucharist was invariably regarded as a sacrifice." Rodatz remarks: "As our Lord shed His blood upon the Cross in atonement for sins, it would be unreasonable to suppose that when He gives it in the Eucharist, He deprives it of its power to atone. The Catholic doctrine of the Eucharist as a sacrifice of atonement has frequently been unfairly criticized by Protestants."

It is therefore a complete mistake to imagine that in the primitive Church there was simply a celebration of Holy Communion, to which at a later date Catholicism added the idea of sacrifice, contrary to the commandment and promise of God. The Catholic Church has at all times with unwavering loyalty adhered to the form of the Eucharist which our Lord Himself committed to the Apostles to be an unbloody sacrifice and the greatest proof of His love.

Priesthood

Protestants recognize no priesthood resembling the Levitical, and say that under the new dispensation Jesus Christ was the one High Priest; and as He procured us access to the Father, there is no longer any need of priests. Moreover, as even Bellarmine acknowledges, there is in the New Testament no mention of priests, but only of ministers, in the Christian Church.

We might therefore say that there ought to be no superintendents, missionaries, Sunday school teachers, etc., because they are not mentioned in the New Testament. There are many allusions to bishops, presbyters, and deacons (1 Tim. iv, 14; v, 22; 2 Tim. i, 6; Titus, 1, 5; Acts xx, 28, etc.). If we really have access to the Father through Christ alone in the sense that all human intermediation must be excluded, why should there be any ministers or preachers? Surely, their object is to bring men into contact with God. Whence do they derive their office, commission, and right to intrude between the soul desirous of salvation and the word of God? Lechler, a Protestant, expressed the opinion that if the Lutheran doctrine of the universal priesthood were taken seriously, the absolute collapse of God's scheme of salvation would be the inevitable result (*Die neutestamentliche Lehre vom heiligen Amt*).

Another question arises here: If priests do not come from Christ, where do they come from? Who was the first to take upon himself the office, and to proclaim to the amazed Church: "I am your priest. I have power to offer Christ's Body and Blood in sacrifice"? If such a man ever had come forward, would there have been no outcry, no opposition? Would not men have died as martyrs rather than take part in a sacrifice that they recognized as contrary to the will of God? Does it not follow that the priesthood must always have been regarded as of divine institution? In the Apostolic age men certainly looked upon it thus, for otherwise why should Simon have offered money for the powers exercised by the Apostles, had he seen in them only what Protestants perceive, and not channels for imparting the Holy Ghost? (cf. Acts viii.) The Catholic Church now regards the priesthood in exactly the same light as St. Clement did in the first century and St. Justin in the second century.

The Renewal of Christ's Sacrifice

Protestants say that they refuse to admit that our Lord commanded the Apostles, and after them the priests of the Church, to sacrifice His

Body and Blood again. Nowhere is it recorded in Holy Scripture that He ordered priests to succeed Him and sacrifice Him as an atonement, but we read that He offered Himself once on the Cross for our sins. The apologists of the Catholic Church are quite aware of this, and at the Council of Trent a proposal was made to declare that the current teaching about the Sacrifice of the Mass was based on tradition alone, since the passages quoted from the Bible really prove nothing, and expose the Church to ridicule on the part of heretics.

Protestants maintain that it is quite contrary to Holy Scripture to regard the Mass as a sacrifice, since the Bible teaches that Christ could not be offered again and again as a victim; nor could He suffer and die more than once, and yet this would be necessary if He were to continue to be offered up in sacrifice. Moreover, His atonement requires no subsequent action to be performed by priests, because it lasts forever (Hebr. x, 12, 14). What can be lacking in Christ's offering, or what can be added to it, if "by one oblation He hath perfected for ever them that are sanctified"? He gives us in Holy Communion the benefit of this oblation; what more is needed? Is not every attempt to supplement it derogatory to His one oblation, and a violation of His sacred rights?

Protestants are careful to avoid making any suggestion as to the origin of the universal Catholic belief in the true, unbloody renewal in Holy Mass of Christ's sacrifice on the Cross. They are at liberty to say that they recognize no sacrifice subsequent to that offered by Christ Himself, but all their protestations and denials are powerless to affect the Mass. The refusal of a party of blind men to believe in the sun's existence could not affect its light. It is a fact that all Catholics believe in the Sacrifice of the Mass, and this faith must have originated somewhere. Did the Apostles receive it from their divine Master and transmit it to the Church? Did He in His infinite love desire His one oblation on the Cross to be presented forever in an unbloody manner in every place where His disciples met together? Was it His design to apply the graces, merited once for all by His death, to all men in every age by means of a visible sacrifice similar to that of the Cross? Did He intend the feast that He instituted on the eve of His Passion to be a sacrifice as well as food? If such were His intentions, it does not behoove His followers to ask, "How can this Man give us His flesh to eat?" (even

Protestants profess to believe that He does this) or, "How can He at the same time cause His flesh and blood to be a true sacrifice?" All that they are required to do is thankfully to accept and faithfully to avail themselves of this priceless benefit.

If, however, the belief in the unbloody Sacrifice of the Mass did not originate with Christ and was not taught by His Apostles, it must have arisen at some unknown time and place, have been invented by some unauthorized person, and foisted upon the Church. Forthwith, without the smallest objection, all the clergy and laity must have accepted this new, unapostolic and unchristian doctrine, so that thenceforth in every place where hitherto only the Lord's Supper had been celebrated, the Sacrifice of the Mass took its place. Something like this must inevitably have occurred if the Holy Sacrifice were indeed unchristian and unapostolic. But we know with absolute certainty that ever since the first Eucharist was celebrated in the Cenaculum at Jerusalem it has been regarded as a sacrifice, and Luther was the first to deny it; we have already seen who instigated him to do this.

Harnack, the Protestant theologian (*Dogmengesch.*, I, 386), admits that in the primitive Church the prophecy of Malachias (i, 11) regarding the clean oblation which should be offered in every place after the Jewish sacrifices had passed away, was always referred to the Holy Eucharist. With regard to the prophecy in Ps. cix, Luther himself says (1556 ed., VIII, 579 b): "The offering of bread and wine by Melchisedech represents the priesthood of Christ from that time to the end of the world, and shows that among Christians He offers the hidden Sacrament of the altar, viz., His sacred Body and precious Blood."

"There are two torrents that amaze me," says Israel Zangwill, the noted Hebrew novelist; "the one is Niagara, and the other the outpouring of reverent prayer falling perpetually in the Roman Catholic Church. What, with Masses and the exposition of the Host, there is no day nor moment of the day in which the praises of God are not being sung somewhere — in noble churches, in dim crypts and underground chapels, in cells and oratories. Niagara is indifferent to spectators, and so the everlasting stream of prayer. As steadfastly and unremittingly as God sustains the universe, so steadfastly and unremittingly is He acknowledged, the human antiphony answering the divine strophe" (*Italian Fantasies*).

The words of institution contain a clear allusion to the sacrificed body and the blood shed for the forgiveness of sins. Christ's Body and Blood possess the property of being sacrifices of atonement, even in the Holy Eucharist. Olshausen, a Protestant, commenting on 1 Cor. x, 18, says of St. Paul, that the Apostle regarded Communion also as a sacrificial banquet, and not merely as a commemoration of Christ's sacrifice on the Cross. With reference to the faith of the primitive Church, we may quote Dr. Grabe, a non-Catholic scholar, who acknowledges that Irenaeus and all the Fathers whose writings are still extant, both the contemporaries of the Apostles and their immediate successors, looked upon the Holy Eucharist as the sacrifice of the new dispensation. The whole Christian Church, not merely some local congregation, accepted this view as originating with Christ and the Apostles.

We know, of course, that Christ does not again suffer or shed blood or die; in fact we call Holy Mass "the unbloody sacrifice." Those who refuse simply to accept Christ's words and works as He uttered and performed them, are forced to make additions and improvements to them; but such is not the intention of the preacher who makes known the word of Christ, nor of any one who administers Baptism in His name, nor is it the intention of the priest celebrating Mass, for it is through his agency that Christ, our eternal High Priest, effects transubstantiation, sacrifices, and gives Holy Communion.

On innumerable occasions has the Catholic Church most solemnly professed her faith in the Holy Sacrifice of the Cross and its infinite value, as well as in Jesus Christ our only Mediator and Redeemer. She has never wavered in this faith, but still she is reproached with undervaluing our Lord's sacrifice and tampering with His rights. Yet she does nothing but represent anew in a mystical manner, according to Christ's will and commission, the sacrifice that He once accomplished with the shedding of blood and that He is ever ready to accomplish. She does this in order that His sacrifice of atonement for the whole world may be applied to each individual soul. Protestants say that Christ confers on' us the benefits of His sacrifice, when we receive His Body and Blood in Holy Communion. This is quite true, but we receive this Communion only from the altar of sacrifice in the Catholic Church. We recognize no other Communion than that which our Lord instituted; we do not venture to separate it from the living tradition through which it has come down to us, and we believe that there can be no Eucharist without priests, regularly ordained and commissioned, or without transubstantiation.

The Office of the Priesthood

As the reason why the papacy upholds this doctrine of the Holy Sacrifice, Protestants state that all the prestige and power and, to a great extent, also the revenues of the papacy and priesthood depend upon it. A priest with authority to celebrate Mass is a mediator and interpreter between God and man. His power transcends all human imagination and nothing on earth is comparable with it. "Who," they ask, "would not fear men who alone are able to give us access to God, and whose authority is supposed to extend beyond the grave?" Young Protestants are warned against yielding to the claims of the priesthood, and are taught that, as it was not instituted by God, it is of no avail. Stipends for Masses are supposed to bring in vast sums of money, and Protestants point with admiration to their own ministers, living in Apostolic poverty, and contrast them with the Catholic priests who are represented as possessing boundless wealth.

There is not much danger at the present day that the young will yield to extravagant claims of the priesthood; they are more likely to adopt the views of those who recognize no distinctions in the civil and ecclesiastical order. Consequently men who still believe it to be God's will that such distinctions should exist, ought to be on their guard against encouraging anarchy by attacking a class of men respected, honoured, and loved by all good Catholics.

Jesus Christ set the twelve Apostles over the rest of the faithful, and conferred upon St. Peter the highest position among them. He intrusted men, holding a special office in the Church, with the task of guarding His grace and doctrine and communicating the same to individuals. Whoever has been admitted into the ranks of clergy by means of episcopal ordination, has a right to say with St. Paul, "Let a man so account of us as of the ministers of Christ, and the dispensers of the mysteries of God" (1 Cor. iv, 1), so great are the treasures confided to his care. St. Paul looked upon himself as a mediator and interpreter between God and man, for he writes to the Corinthians (*ib.* 15, 16), "In Christ Jesus by the Gospel I have begotten you; wherefore I beseech you, be ye followers of me, as I also am of Christ." Apparently he opened to his converts a means of access to God.

Has not every Protestant minister the intention of doing the same, although he cannot claim to be the officially appointed steward of the mysteries of God? A Catholic priest is not, in the eyes of his people, an intruder between them and God, nor does he lead them to God by his personal qualities, his knowledge, or his goodness, but simply in his official capacity as the servant of God and His Church. He has not assumed this office, nor is he appointed to exercise functions of human origin, but, as the servant of Christ, to whom alone he is answerable, he uses the authority intrusted to him in the name of God. A Protestant minister expounds his own views or those taught him by his professors, and frequently, since he is a state official, his teaching is contrary to God's revelation. He is under civil control, and in some places his superior can alter the established religion, or invent a new one, if he chooses, so that a minister ceases to do anything more than teach morals, draw up statistics, or even act as an agent of the police (cf. Gebhardt, *Thüringische Kirchengeschichte*, 1882, part 2, p. 225).

A Catholic priest holds a dignified and sacred office, but he and his people know in whose name and authority he exercises it, and for what end. Hence he must not misuse it in order to obtain "prestige, power, and revenues." In the sight of God a priest is an unworthy servant to whose charge something sacred is intrusted, and by whom a strict account will have to be rendered. Fearful indeed will be his sentence, if he misuses his office and talents for his own advancement or for his temporal advantage. Protestants are fond of quoting the Roman Catechism, but they overlook a statement that it contains, to the effect that those who become priests solely to obtain food and clothing commit the grievous sin of sacrilege, although it is right that "they that serve the altar, partake with the altar" (1 Cor. ix, 13). No man could commit a meaner or more contemptible sin than to become a priest through ambition or for the sake of money. He would deserve to be classed with Judas. It is undeniable that even among the servants of Christ there have always been abuses which have done much harm to the Church; but the Church as a whole cannot be held responsible for the faults of individual priests any more than the Apostles can be blamed for the sin of Judas. Are there no Protestant ministers who exercise their office as a means of acquiring honour or worldly goods? Did not Luther accept a barrel of wine and express most profound gratitude for it to Philip of Hesse, who sent it in return for his advice to marry two wives? (Lenz, *Briefwechsel Landgraf Philipps*, p. 361, etc.)

Mass and Sermon

Protestants profess to be very uneasy regarding the danger to souls resulting from the Mass. It appears to them disastrous that by this human ordinance men are distracted from the study of God's word. They say that if we only hear the words of the Mass (which, being in Latin, are unintelligible to most people), we fulfil our obligation of hearing Mass on Sunday; we are not ordered but only advised to hear a sermon.

The Holy Sacrifice of the Mass is not and cannot be a human ordinance, for in that case it would never have been accepted by the Church in every age and place. The sacrifice does not distract Catholics from the study of God's word, nor is it an obstacle preventing them from coming to God; it is, on the contrary, the best possible means of leading them to Him if they unite themselves in spirit with the actions and prayers of the priest. Catholics are taught what the sacrifice is and what it signifies, and so they can follow it with love and devotion, believing that the oblation, once offered by Christ on the Cross, is renewed in an unbloody manner on the altar. Each is free to pray as he desires, in accordance with his personal needs; he is not bound to listen to the priest, but may use his own words and participate in the sacrifice as his own feelings may prompt him, for wherever he is in the world he understands what is going on at Mass.

It is false to say that by simply listening to the words of the Mass a Catholic fulfils all his obligations. The Church requires him to assist at the Holy Sacrifice with reverence and devotion; she says nothing about listening to words uttered by the priest. The sacrifice, and not the sermon, is the chief part of our public worship, but any Protestant minister must know that the preaching of God's word is by no means neglected in Catholic churches. The sermon cannot indeed take the place of the sacrifice but it has always accompanied it; and to hear a sermon is a duty for all who cannot otherwise obtain the necessary instruction. Parish priests are bound to preach, in accordance with God's commandment (*Conc. Trid.*, sess. 23, cap. 1). It is not easy to see how Protestants are more strictly ordered to hear sermons than we are.

The Fruits of the Mass

Protestants bring very serious charges against Holy Mass itself. They say that according to Catholic doctrine, on account of this sacrifice offered by a priest, God forgives even terrible offences, sins are blotted out, punishment is remitted, satisfaction is made, and assistance is given to all the faithful, living and dead (*Conc. Trid.*, XXII, c. 2). This is why hundreds of Masses are said for the souls of the wealthy and aristocratic, and even the poor do their best to pay for Masses for the dead. Then there is the use of privileged altars, i.e., altars on which the Pope has conferred the special privilege, that every time Mass is said at them a soul is released from purgatory. Protestants congratulate themselves upon avoiding the "broad way" of papal indulgences and Masses, and say that they bear in mind our Saviour's words: "Narrow is the gate, and strait is the way, that leadeth to life, and few there are that find it" (Matth. vii, 14).

The statement given above is a misrepresentation and mutilation of the teaching of the Council of Trent which declared the Mass to be a sacrifice of atonement, because in it the same Christ is offered in an unbloody manner, who offered Himself and shed His Blood on the altar of the Cross. Therefore God forgives even terrible offences for the sake of Christ's sacrifice, not on account of anything done by the priest. The Council declared explicitly that mercy and pardon are bestowed upon those who draw near to God with sincerity and steadfast faith, with fear and reverence, and with humble and penitent hearts. Plainly, therefore, it is not enough simply to hear Mass, and it is unfair on the part of people professing to give an account of Catholic teaching to misrepresent it so grossly. To sinners who come to Him with the required dispositions, God, being reconciled by this sacrifice, applies the merits gained once for all by Christ on Calvary, and in this way they obtain forgiveness of even grievous sins, since grace and the gift of true contrition are given them. Such is the teaching of the Catholic Church, and according to it, she requires far more of a sinner than Luther did, for he promised the most plenary indulgence imaginable, in life and in death, to all who have faith, and taught that faith alone without any penance whatever can deliver from the most infamous sins, both in this life and the next. Is Luther's gate narrower and his way more strait than that of the Catholic Church? Non-Catholics have a deeply rooted objection to Masses for the dead; yet they are as ancient as the Mass itself, and St. John Chrysostom traces the memento of the faithful departed in the Mass back to the Apostles themselves (*Hom. in Matth.*). Tertullian speaks of the custom of offering Mass on the anniversary of a death as very ancient. St. Cyril of Jerusalem says: "We believe that it affords great relief to the souls of the departed, if we pray for them whilst the holy and awful sacrifice offered for them rests upon the altar. We wreathe no garlands for them, but we offer Christ, sacrificed for our sins, when we make atonement on their behalf and our own to God, who loves mankind" (*Catech. myst.*, 5, 9). It is, therefore, a very ancient Christian custom to remember the dead at the altar; but God alone can decide how far each individual soul is capable and susceptible of grace. We are convinced, however, that souls capable of being helped derive great assistance and consolation from the Holy Sacrifice, in which the Church offers our heavenly Father the most precious atonement for the sins of the whole world. The Holy Sacrifice is more efficacious than prayer, almsgiving, and other works of piety and love; but we cannot tell to what extent the sufferings of any individual soul are mitigated or shortened by a Mass said on its behalf. Nothing has been revealed or promised on the subject, and the Catholic Church has never taught that a soul is delivered from purgatory whenever Mass is said at a privileged altar; nor does she make the way to heaven easier for the rich than for the poor. How could she possibly do so when she recommends her children to practise evangelical poverty, and does her utmost to remind the rich and powerful of their duties and responsibilities? She regards rich and poor as bound by the same laws, and as treading the same path to heaven. The Mass said for a Pope or an emperor differs in no respect from that said for a beggar. It is by God's permission that the wealthy possess more abundant earthly resources, which they can employ either in serving the world or in making to themselves friends who will receive them at the last day. But whoever has great possessions will be called upon to give an account of them, and the Church has never taught that money entitles a man to sin in this world and gives him an advantage over his poorer brother even in the world to come. Rich and poor alike can be saved only through God's grace and their own faithful coöperation with the same, — there is no other way. Lazarus, the beggar, who endures his hard lot patiently for love of God, will in the next life enjoy greater consolation than Dives, who relies on prayers and Masses to be said after his death. It is one thing to desire to help the suffering souls by means of our sacrifices and intercession, and it is quite another to rely upon such things for our own happiness after death. Any one who does this, acts in an unchristian and uncatholic spirit.

Communion under One Kind

The last charge brought by Protestants against the Catholic administration of the Holy Eucharist is that it withholds the consecrated chalice from the laity. Leo I and Gelasius, two very eminent bishops, condemned as heretics those who refused to receive the chalice, and Paschal II (died 1118) wrote that, with regard to the reception of our Lord's Body and Blood, it was not lawful to depart from Christ's own rule, for He gave both bread and wine to His disciples. The Roman party, predominant at the Council of Trent, insisted upon withdrawing the chalice from the laity, and it has never again been restored in spite of the requests of clergy and secular monarchs. The alleged reason for this withdrawal is that if the chalice were given to the laity, they might fall into the error of supposing themselves to be as worthy as the priests to receive the sacrament. This reason was suggested by Gerson at Constance. A Roman Catholic priest remarks however: "If a father were to assemble his household, take a cup and say to his sons, 'Drink ye all of this,' he would not mean that the servants also were to drink of it. Hence Christ's words apply only to the priesthood, whilst servants and handmaids must be satisfied with the bread."

Some zealous Catholics, such as Möhler and Hirscher, demanded the restoration of the chalice. The despised laity of the present day are hardly aware of the deprivation that they suffer in consequence of the "great robbery," — for thus Gelasius describes the separation of the two parts of the Eucharist.

Even in the primitive Church many people received Communion under one kind alone (Basil, *ep*. 93; Tertull., *ad uxor.*, 2, 5), especially the sick, prisoners, children, hermits, and all who communicated in their own homes. In the fourth century the Manicheans came from Africa to Rome, where they mingled with the Catholics and even went with them to Holy Communion. They never received the consecrated wine, because they regarded all wine as evil and abominated it. If at that time Communion in both kinds had been universal they could never have escaped detection, and it was in order to prevent them from approaching the altar that Leo I and Gelasius I commanded all to communicate under both species. When the latter Pope speaks of an intolerable sacrilege, he is not referring to Communion under one kind, but to the superstitious idea that no one ought to communicate under the species of wine.

The Council of Trent did not abandon the teaching of the primitive Church, nor did it condemn Communion under both kinds as sinful or unchristian, but it decided, for very adequate reasons, that henceforth Communion should be administered under one kind alone. The Catholic Church permitted the use of the chalice to nations that asked for it, provided they professed their belief (1) that reception under one kind was sufficient for all except the celebrant, (2) that Christ is present, whole and entire under one, as under two forms, (3) that the Church does not err in administering the Holy Eucharist under one form only to all except the celebrant. But, as Pope Benedict XIV points out (*de sacrif. miss.*, I, n. 367 sq), it seems that the nations which demanded the chalice for the laity, did so either as a pretext for rebellion against the Church or because they mistakenly supposed Communion under one kind alone to be insufficient. In 1564, at the request of the Emperor Ferdinand I, Pius IV actually sanctioned giving the chalice to the laity, but the inhabitants of Catholic countries refused to avail themselves of this permission, and in other regions it gave rise to so many abuses that Pius V and Gregory XIV felt obliged to withdraw it (Wilmers, *Lehrb. d. Relig.*, III, § 61).

Nothing but the bitterest hostility could suggest that an overweening arrogance of the priesthood was the cause of the regulations now in force on the subject of Communion under one kind. Gerson is said to have remarked that if the chalice were given to the laity they might fall into the error of supposing themselves to be as worthy as the priests to receive the sacrament. Gerson gives excellent reasons for Communion under one kind; the laity are not regarded as less worthy than the priests to receive the sacrament. Every priest before communicating strikes his breast, saying, "Lord, I am not worthy," and when he communicates without saying Mass, he receives, like a layman, only a consecrated host. Gerson's words are misinterpreted, and his real meaning is that laymen do not hold the same office in the Church as priests (*Dignitas* is not "worthiness," but "dignity"). Still less suitable is the explanation that the laity are regarded as servants and handmaids, who must be satisfied with bread alone, whilst wine is given to the sons to drink. This is far from being the case; kings and princes, bishops and popes, children and beggars receive from the same holy table the same heavenly food, not bread and wine, but Christ, with His flesh and Blood, His Body and Soul, His divinity and humanity. If a Catholic priest ever made such an explanation, he can only have meant that Communion under both kinds is not required by the words of institution.

The laity are not despised by the Church, who administers her sacraments for their sake as well as for that of the priests. They certainly are not aware of having suffered any great wrong in being "robbed" of the consecrated chalice, because they have never been prevented from receiving the true Eucharistic Communion which is infinitely more than any Protestant receives, for his minister can give him nothing but bread and wine; although if he be truly contrite for his sins, and communicate in sincere faith and love, he may to some extent participate in the graces of a spiritual communion. He cannot really consume the Body and Blood of Christ, because there is no one authorized to do for him what Christ commanded. If any one is so credulous as to believe that Luther gave back to the laity the chalice because they had been robbed of it by papal intrigue, and in restoring it was motived solely by zeal for souls, he should read the *Formula of Mass and Communion for the Church in Wittenberg* (*Works*, Jen. III, 338). Luther writes: "No one is to maintain that they clamour for a Council, at which both species might be restored to them. We have the right of Christ . . . Yes, we assert that if a Council should order or permit this, we should then least of all accept both species; in fact we should show our contempt for the Council and its decision by receiving either one species, or none at all, but certainly not both, and we should utterly curse all who received both species on the authority of such a Council or its decision." Surely such a statement can be the outcome of nothing but the spirit of contradiction!

Impartial Protestants appreciate the Catholic reasons for what is called "withholding the chalice." It is well known that a movement has been started in Protestant circles to prevent the harm resulting from giving the cup to the laity, and in some places proposals have been made for its complete withdrawal.

Made in the USA
Lexington, KY
29 August 2017